Unleashing Your

SUPERPOWER

ADKID
GRAB YUR CAPE!

Unleashing Your

SUPERPOWER

WHY *PERSUASIVE COMMUNICATION IS THE ONLY FORCE YOU WILL EVER NEED.*

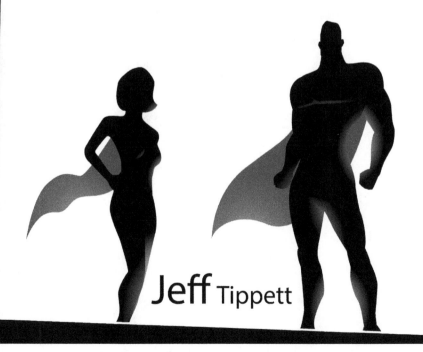

Jeff Tippett

UNLEASHING YOUR SUPERPOWER

The opinions expressed by the author are not necessarily those of
Wisdom House Books, Inc.

Published by Wisdom House Books, Inc.
Chapel Hill, North Carolina 27514 USA
1.919.883.4669 | www.wisdomhousebooks.com

Wisdom House Books is committed to excellence in the publishing industry.

Book design copyright © 2019 by Wisdom House Books, Inc. All rights reserved.

Cover and Interior design by Ted Ruybal

Published in the United States of America

Paperback ISBN: 978-1-7335338-0-5
LCCN: 2018914984

1. SEL040000   SELF-HELP / Communication & Social Skills
2. SEL027000   SELF-HELP / Personal Growth / Success
3. SEL023000   SELF-HELP / Personal Growth / Self-Esteem

First Edition
14 13 12 11 10 / 10 9 8 7 6 5 4 3 2 1

TABLE OF CONTENTS

Chapter 1

THE MEANS TO PERSUADE

"I think the power of persuasion would be the greatest superpower of all time."

—Jenny Mollen—

*I*f you could have any one superpower, what would you choose?

As a kid, I wondered this all the time. Perhaps too much. The ability to fly? The ability to simply mention money, and it would appear? Control minds?

I could never settle. Just when I thought I'd decided, the abilities of another superhero would catch my attention. But each of them had limitations.

What about you? What superpower would you choose?

Well, I finally found mine. My superpower is persuasive communications.

And my bold declaration is this: We all live or die based on our ability to persuade.

Think about it: Everyone needs to persuade. Whether you're

a CEO of a growing firm, a manager with direct responsibility for the performance of those you lead, a salesperson whose income is directly related to your ability to close the sale, or simply an individual hoping to live life with the company of a significant other, we all have to persuade. But how effective are you? And could you do a better job of persuading—and creating better results—for those around you?

So how do you go about developing this power? It's not as daunting as it seems. Here's my audacious promise. If you will take in, determine how they work for you, and apply the concepts that I'm going to share with you, you will:

1. Increase your effectiveness.

2. Have a powerful new tool to help you reach your goals.

3. Positively impact your organization or business.

These concepts are tested and proven. They produce results. And they will work for you.

I want you to win.

I believe in creating and riding waves. But not just for myself. I love seeing others win, as well. I believe that many of you reading this book have great ideas. You have the calling to change circumstances for great numbers of people. Maybe you lead a nonprofit or are a fundraiser or a politician. Whatever it is you do, you'll only be successful when you persuade others to join you on your journey.

You've probably watched, with admiration, as someone persuades others and ultimately creates a win for everyone involved. I hope you've wondered what the secret sauce is that's driving this person's success.

Maybe it's the politician who captures her audience. Banners are raised. People are smiling and cheering. Constituents are motivated, and they turn out to vote.

We've all seen people like Barack Obama who can stand before an arena of people, inspiring them to feel hope, urging them onward, moving them to tears, and compelling them to join him on a journey to bring change. He was able to persuade enough people to come along that he was elected president twice.

On the other hand, you've also seen the politician who just can't quite connect with an audience. Though they seem to want to get behind him, they, instead, go home scratching their heads. He failed to connect.

Maybe you've been in a meeting with your CEO. The company is going through a major transition. And although it's a positive one, you and your colleagues aren't on board. You feel the CEO is only out for herself. The message is wrong.

Another CEO facing the same challenge has the entire room on its feet. They're motivated. They're excited about the change, and they roll up their sleeves, ready to make it happen.

Maybe it's the entrepreneur who's looking for funders. How does he convince them to come along? Maybe it's your pastor, making a convincing case for salvation.

Here's some encouragement: Winning through persuasion isn't for a select few. It's for anyone who's willing to hone the right skills and put them to work. It doesn't take a Barack Obama to stir people into action. Maybe we all can't move an entire nation, but we can hone the skills that it takes to determine and better articulate what we say, how we structure it, how we voice it—how we pull people along on a mutually advantageous journey.

Life isn't a pie with limited slices. Life is a huge buffet, with more dishes being perpetually added.

But you have to want it and be willing to thoroughly think it through.

ооо

I'd now like to tell you a little about myself and why I'm writing this book.

Growing up, I was always a go-get-it kind of kid. My mother was forever admonishing me to, "Settle down, Jeffery. Settle down."

But it made no sense to me. It just didn't register. Why settle down when there was so much to be done—so much to discover? Why settle down when there were so many cool things I could be out there doing?

Yep, I was that kid. From as far back as I can remember, I've wanted to be out there making something happen.

By the time I'd entered elementary school, I was in hyperdrive.

The most common comments on my report card were: "Jeff continues to talk too much in class." "Jeff has a hard time sitting still in his seat." I was that Ritalin kid who the teachers prayed—prayed each day—had taken his meds.

I felt pressures, both internal and external. My parents expected me to earn good grades. It wasn't a wish, it was a mandate. And though I started out with the impression that good grades were dependent upon my homework, quizzes, tests—quantifiable things—I learned, in time, that there was another equally important factor: my teacher's impressions of me. I worked at making a more positive impression, and I know it made a difference.

Outside the classroom, I was always looking for the next big thing. I wanted to be at the head of the pack.

One of my earliest memories of persuading other kids to follow me was when I was eight or so, leading my friends through the neighborhood woods with torches we'd devised and, not surprisingly, accidentally setting a small fire. Fortunately, we were able to put it out ourselves. What a rush it was, charging forward, ablaze. I suppose there's a metaphor there.

I think my DNA is hardwired for entrepreneurship. From an early age, I was on the hunt for business opportunities. Yard work was an early opportunity. But I wasn't content with simply mowing lawns. Instead, I landed the "contracts," and then hired my friends to do the work. It was called Snoopy's Yard Service.

In the spring, I would knock on my neighbors' doors to see if they wanted their lawn mowed, and in the fall, see if they wanted someone to rake up their leaves. I even created little yard signs that I set up with scraps that my father, who was in the construction business, would have around.

My friends wanted work, and I had it. And now I was in business. I had a consistent revenue stream, steady clients. I was putting people to work, and now I was free to do other things.

I'd pay everyone enough to be happy and keep a share for myself. There were things I wanted to buy, and I liked the idea of saving.

I was the rainmaker—or whatever the eleven-year-old version of rainmaker would be. I'd shaken the bushes and secured the work.

My first real job, my first W2, was cleaning up a radio station at night and on weekends. Over time, I got to know the owners, and landed a job as a weekend DJ. I had a *real* job.

I'm a classically trained pianist, and at fifteen, I got my first church gig, playing organ during services. Now I was really generating revenue.

I finished high school a year early, but at about the same time, I encountered a detour. My father had a run-in with the minister of the church where I was playing—and where I was also active in the youth group, and dating that minister's daughter—and he gave me an ultimatum: either leave the church or leave the house. I left the house.

I was seventeen; I packed my things and found a place to live. I was supporting myself with two or three jobs. Making it happen required quite a bit persuasion of all kinds.

I was learning how to make things happen. Whatever it was that needed to happen—a place to live, income—I was finding a way to make it happen.

Though I never paused to think about it for long at the time, I can say now that, at times, I thought something was wrong with me. Why was I always starting something new? Why couldn't I just settle for average? Why couldn't I just be calm like everyone around me? Why was I always stirring something up?

Only when I embraced who I am, and came to love what made me different, did I realize that there's a reason I am who I am. The passion and drive were in me for a reason. I had value to bring to others.

So now we're at the moment I've been building to.

It was late June of 2003. My father, with whom I'd reconciled, had just returned from a mission trip to Haiti. We were to meet at a restaurant to hear about his trip and look at his pictures. Though I wish I could say I was anxiously awaiting the details of his trip, I was more excited that we were meeting at a barbeque restaurant I liked.

There was nothing unusual about our dinner until he pulled out the photographs of his trip. Among them was one of a baby. A baby just months old. And this baby needed a home. Now everything changed. Forever.

Her looking into my eyes—it ignited something within me.

Why was I drawn to this picture? How did I know deep inside that I was the one the universe had chosen to be her father? I had never considered adoption. I had a three-year-old daughter and a five-month-old son. The last thing I needed was two babies at once.

If you know anything about international adoptions, you know they can be rough. The travel, learning the way business is done in another country; the wear on the emotions, determination and finances. This adoption was no different. In fact, the struggle was escalated since President Jean-Bertrand Aristide's government was collapsing.

The government falling apart compounded the already difficult tasks of an international adoption. I remember getting an email from my attorney, informing me that the adoptions offices were shut down, with no indication of when they would reopen.

My adoption was now on hold. But something inside me couldn't accept this reality. Within a couple of days, I was back in Haiti. My plan was to walk to that office every morning, hoping someone would happen to come in, even though the office wasn't officially open.

So for days, I did just that. Every morning, I would walk to the office. I would sit there all day, then return to my attorney's home each night, empty handed.

Until one day. One day, someone showed.

You can likely imagine how pent up I was when this official finally showed. My emotions were on edge, and I didn't have many English-speaking people around for me to vent. Once I finally had an audience with this official, I spouted out all my demands of what he should do for me. My approach was to make this official do what I wanted—regardless of what that took. My story was filled with words like "I," "me," and "my."

And this official told me, "No."

I knew I had to reframe my messaging—quickly. I had to get this on track. Drawing from what I had learned about Haitians, I knew they loved their children. They viewed them as jewels.

So, I changed my approach. I began to talk about this Haitian baby that didn't have a home, no financial resources, no promise of education or love.

And instantly, this government official changed his mind. Within ten minutes, my paper was signed, and I was on my way.

I reflected on what had just transpired my entire walk back to my attorney's home.

Up to this point, I thought my archenemy was the deteriorating Haitian bureaucracy. I viewed the government as the obstacle keeping me from accomplishing my worthy goal of adopting this baby. After all, employees of the government rarely showed up for work, and were uncooperative when they did. The unrest within the government was prompting people to riot, creating life-threatening situations I had never encountered. As a result of this complete dysfunction, I felt that the entire government was against me. And I had to take down this enemy.

But walking back to my Haitian attorney's house, I couldn't help but ponder what had happened. The government official went from blockage to compliance. What changed? Why did he first say no, then say yes?

I had built a solid reputation for getting things done. If the job needed to be completed—no matter how complicated—just get Jeff on board. He'd get it done. But what if that meant I was a master manipulator, determined to get my way no matter the cost or consequence to others?

Although I wanted to blame the government, what I now knew was that I was my own enemy. My general mode of operation was to manipulate. I was focused on my desires without any consideration of my audience. And, here, that had been the wrong approach.

While this understanding didn't immediately change my approach to communication, it did start the process of understanding that I needed to change. Because if I wanted to find sustainable approaches to moving others, I couldn't manipulate. I had to persuade.

And as a result of this lesson, my stalled adoption was back on track.

Even with this victory, nothing was easy about this adoption. I had to take multiple trips to Haiti. I became ill during travel. Right before Christmas, we were told the adoption was completed, only to then learn that it wasn't. It was a tough Christmas. The newly decorated bedroom of our daughter-to-be remained empty throughout what was supposed to be the most joyous season of the year.

Then in January, another call came. The paperwork was finished. This crazy ordeal was about to end. I was going to be a father to a third child. Words couldn't describe my excitement. I packed immediately and flew back to Haiti, arriving fully expecting to leave the next day with a beautiful baby girl.

I picked her up from her caregiver, but I barely recognized her. She had lost a lot of weight. She was extremely sick with a double ear infection and a nasty stomach virus. I was hell-bent on getting her out quickly. I even considered trying to get a return flight that same day.

I carried her in my arms. Her head was limp; she was vomiting. She had terrible diarrhea. And she was denied a visa. She was flagged for a DNA test. For the first time throughout this entire extended process, I felt totally defeated. I was in Port-au-Prince. Alone. Holding a baby so sick she couldn't hold her head up. I pleaded. But to no avail.

I called back to the States and had a friend reach out to my senator. His office offered compassion and a willingness to help. And finally, we were able to get her a visa.

The flight back was horrendous. Nina screamed the entire time from Port-au-Prince to Miami. The cabin pressure was adding additional pain to her fragile, infected ears. Upon our arrival, standing alone in the airport with this sick infant, I finally felt a sense of accomplishment. My six-and-a-half-month journey to adopt a baby from Haiti ended with success. I was happy and proud.

And then out of this feeling of accomplishment came a spark of recognition, and a question arose: "What changes would now ensue as a result of having persuaded dozens of people that I was the perfect dad for this little girl?"

I now began to question how her life would be different. Could she accomplish things that wouldn't have otherwise been possible? Will she be a doctor? Will she become a nurse? Will she go back to Haiti? Who knows what lies ahead?

What lives will she affect on her journey? How would my life change?

Though I didn't have the answers, I knew they would be revealed over time. What I did know was that my ability to persuade wasn't the end game. It simply triggered a domino effect that would lead who knows where. A greater good, I felt, was set in motion. And it began with my commitment to persuade.

I'd now completed my checklist of the things necessary to secure this adoption. It had been wrenching. But it was done.

And it was now just the beginning. All that was over. But that was nothing. Now the real work lay ahead—raising Nina.

What I saw for the first time was that each step of this initial journey—each encounter that had required persuasion—had allowed me to accomplish the task at hand—which was the launch of something much bigger.

I walked out of Immigration in the Miami airport with Nina now sleeping in my arms. I paused. I looked at her. I reflected on the past six and a half months and felt the tears fill my eyes. The feeling of accomplishment was overshadowed by a greater understanding. Throughout the process, I had dozens of people I needed to make respond in my favor. This adoption could not have happened on my own. I needed others to do what was best. This journey had taught me that I don't have to accept what is. I can persuade. I can affect change.

My ability to get things done was limited; every success was dependent upon my actions. Every step was dependent on coaxing others to action.

In this book, I'll be guiding you in crafting a captivating message and developing an irresistible call to action. What I hope to convey is that, whatever it is you're trying to accomplish—whether it's policy you're trying to move forward, a business deal you're striving to seal, or an election you're trying to win—

it isn't just about this one moment. It's about the unknown that lies ahead—the possibilities it opens up—that wouldn't, couldn't, have happened if you hadn't employed the powers of persuasion.

Now everything lies ahead—the unknown, the potential.

And it clicked for me in that moment in the Miami airport. Up until then, the checklist was the objective. Now, I realized this was no longer it. All of this was toward a greater good. I want you to see that it's almost always about more than the immediate task at hand—that all such things lead to something much bigger.

The first time I really knew it was all going to be okay was one day when Nina was about three. She was sitting in the floor arranging different toys, and I asked her what she was doing. She said she was making families. "They don't all match," she said, "but they're still a family. Just like I don't match, but we're still a family."

What a feeling that was. So much lay ahead.

It's not like anything has yet been completed. There's no nicely wrapped package. It's an awareness that starts a spark, leads to the next, and then the next. It just gets bigger and bigger.

Bottom line: This isn't about the quick win. It's not about selling one car and you're done. It's about how we approach life, in all its aspects. It's about how each little win can lead to transformational change.

I'm going to be asking you to embrace the power of persuasion—to open yourself to its full potential.

Some people view the world as a pie—there are a limited number of slices, and once they're gone, the pie is no more. I'm more of a banquet-table guy myself. The more people that come to dinner, the better. We can always pull up another chair.

The greatest success I can hope for with this book will be if you tell me you've experienced a win. That you persuaded people along your journey. While you may master some of the tips in this book, if you close its back cover and have just one new tool in your arsenal, I believe it will be worth the read. Just one minor shift of a rudder can move a boat in a whole new direction.

Again, I don't think persuasion is about one-off wins. I think it's about mindset. It's a mindset to forever strive to win.

So you've made it through the introduction with me. I'd now like to ask you to proceed with me through these chapters, and then to begin to practice it all on your own. Why start, if you're not going to finish? And why finish, if you're not going to put the skills to practice?

To paraphrase Aristotle, "We need the means to persuade." This book gives you those means.

Let's do this!

Questions for Reflection

1. What does "superpower" mean to you?

2. If you were performing more effectively, what areas of your life would improve?

3. What goals are in front of you right now?

4. Given the opportunity, what would you positively impact in your company?

5. I've shared my Haitian adoption story. What life story has greatly impacted your life?

Chapter 2

MANIPULATION VS. PERSUASION

"Not brute force but only persuasion and faith are the kings of this world."

—Thomas Carlyle—

First, I'd like to make an important distinction.

When I talk with people about my area of expertise in persuasive communications, a common first response is some variation of, "Oh, you teach people how to manipulate others?"

It's an understandable response. After all, most people have likely seen more instances of manipulation than persuasion. And most training on persuasion is really just good ol' manipulation. So it's not their fault they don't grasp the difference. You might not, either.

Let's first talk about manipulation.

Encyclopedia.com defines manipulation as: "to control or influence (a person or situation) cleverly, unfairly, or unscrupulously."

Yikes! Who wants that?

Some popular synonyms are "control," "exploit," and "gerry-mander." Like the definition, none of these are palatable to me. I doubt to you, either.

So why do people manipulate?

First, I think manipulation is easier. Persuasion takes a lot of work. It takes a commitment from you to work on your messaging, to learn how to frame, and position and ask. And it demands that the other person have respect for you.

Manipulation aligns with our core of too often being more concerned about ourselves than others. When we manipulate, our actions are self-centered.

Manipulation works—at least for short-term applications. That's right, manipulation does often successfully influence others. But it comes at a cost. That cost is your integrity and the forfeiture of an opportunity for long-term success. Most of us could get on a sales call and use crafty language, direct force, and pushiness to make a sale. But, likely, that'll be the final sale with that person. We know that among the most substantial costs in business is customer acquisition, and that retention is a much better option than repeatedly having to find new customers.

I think of my experiences with gyms and fitness centers. You know how it goes—you sign up for a new gym, and they offer your first session with a trainer for free. Well, nothing in life is free. And the price you'll likely pay for that "free" session is manipulation to get you to sign up for a complete training package. And the pressure won't stop anytime soon. The calls and emails continue. Relentlessly.

A final reason I think we often resort to manipulation is that we've become conditioned to it; we've learned it through our experiences with others. If I asked you to raise your hand if you've ever been manipulated, it's likely every hand would go up. Through personal experience, others have taught us to manipulate as they strove for what they wanted.

But enough of the negative! Let's talk persuasion.

Persuasion is defined as: "to cause (someone) to do something through reasoning or argument." The word "argument" here refers more to the original definition of two people presenting a logical reasoning of their perspective. This is not your family Thanksgiving dinner, with everyone discussing politics or religion.

Let's look at the etymology of the word "persuasion." It comes from the Latin *persuadere*, which can be broken down into two parts: *per*, meaning through or to completion; and *suadere*, which means to advise.

So persuasion, at its root, means to move people by advising them. You're leading them to believe something—which means they now accept this knowledge as their own. In other words, in using all the tools and techniques we're about to discuss in this book, persuasion is helping people come to the same understanding you have, and to believe it for themselves and on their own.

Now that's powerful!

How do you know when you've reached that point? Well, I believe there are two words you'll likely hear from the other person: "That's right." When you hear those two words, you can rest assured you've avoided manipulation. Rather, the two of you have arrived at the same conclusion.

You've been persuasive.

Another industry expert's perspective:

> When I reflect on the past fifty years of my life, there have been three core aspects of my character that have been vital to any success I enjoyed during that period: candor, passion, and persuasion.
>
> I attribute my candor and directness to my mother's influence, thanks in part to her lineage to the hard-working Calabrese who later immigrated to Brazil. It has served me well when earning trust. My passion is simply innate and perhaps a product of having Portuguese, Brazilian, and Italian heritage. Combined with my candor, I've noticed that it's hard for others not to get swept up by the strong emotions I feel for one thing or the other.
>
> I'm convinced that my ability to persuade is that much stronger because of my candor and passion. That's because persuasion, unlike manipulation, is established through

reasoning or argument and is more successful when conveyed with honest emotion and directness. I have won many new business pitches as a result of this level of persuasive communications. Another example of this in practice are trial attorneys making opening and closing arguments to a jury. I'm sure you've seen examples of this on television or in film—the attorney persuades the jury by delivering the facts with great passion. However, persuasion's arch-enemy, manipulation, is often used in the same courtroom scenario and can be hard to differentiate from.

Over the years, advertising has been accused of manipulating consumers, and rightly so. If you go back to the archived ads of the 40s, 50s, and 60s, you'll find outrageous claims and promises made. Not only would advertisers tell you their brand or product was better than their competitors with little to no proof, but they would even go so far as to suggest they could deliver unrealistic benefits to the consumer and their way of life. Perhaps the primary offenders were the cigarette manufacturers. A 1946 ad for Camels stated, "More doctors smoke Camels than any other cigarette." Tipalet's ad in 1969 even goes so far as objectifying women to successfully manipulate consumers with its headline, "Blow in her face and she'll follow you anywhere."

Fortunately, consumers today are more aware of false claims. They conduct independent research before making impulsive and uneducated purchasing decisions, thanks to the Internet. As a person who has never practiced in manipulation, this makes me very happy. You may think that advertising agencies wish to help sell brands and products at all costs. Not true. It's my belief that brands should conduct their businesses ethically and produce great products that deliver on consumer demands and make their lives better, as a result. Ultimately, an advertiser's job is to communicate this information in the most persuasive way possible. Could advertisers use manipulation tactics, instead? Of course, but it wouldn't be long until it became evident to the consumers and they became distrustful of those advertisers forever.

Wágner dos Santos,
thewagner.agency

Questions for Reflection

1. Compare and contrast manipulation and persuasion as you view them. How are they similar, and how are they different?

2. Can you think of times in which you know you manipulated someone? If so, think through those, including how you felt and how you perceived the other person felt.

3. Can you think of times in which you know you persuaded someone? If so, how did you know? And what was the outcome?

4. When you are on the receiving end, can you tell the difference when someone is trying to persuade you? Or manipulate you? How do the two feel? And how do you feel about the person?

5. Do you think there are ever times when manipulation is a better option to accomplish what you want? Or is persuasion always the best option?

Chapter 3

SIMPLE MESSAGE

"If you can't explain something simply, you don't know enough about it."

—Albert Einstein —

Whether conveying a policy position, business concepts, or the attributes of a product—whatever it is you need to share in order to pull your audience along—no one will jump on board if they don't clearly grasp your message. Almost all effective, persuasive messaging has one common core component: simplicity.

But here's the thing: If you don't capture them quickly, you'll lose them forever. You have seconds to capture your audience. If they can't quickly—as in *seconds*—grasp your core message, you're sure to lose them. And if you don't capture them at the get-go, you're not likely to regain their attention.

There's been a lot of research recently on the complexity of language and people's attention spans. This book isn't designed to explore, dissect, and/or validate this research. But I do think it's fair to assert that reading comprehension is on the decline and attention spans are growing shorter.

Most people don't read, they scan. And they gravitate toward stylistic devices like bullet points that offer simple content and lots of white space. That's how we grab people these days.

We can express disappointment, advocate for change all day long, but at least for now, we have to accept that, if you want to persuade, you need to structure your content succinctly. You need to craft simple, impactful messaging.

In later chapters, we'll discuss how to select and structure language that persuades. But for now, let's focus on how to craft simple messaging.

First and foremost is making certain your core message is easily accessible to your audience—that you're using language that isn't unnecessarily busy. We've established that the message is rarely simple; it is, in most cases, multifaceted. And you probably know the issue at its deepest and most complex level. You probably know every intricacy. And you should.

But when it comes to persuading others, you must—at least at the outset—keep it simple. Here are some suggestions to help with that.

1. DEBRIEF YOURSELF

When I set about to craft a message, ideas begin to bounce around my head like ping-pong balls. I see all the dimensions, curves, angles, various components. I've now got to get all that out of my head, to make some record of it.

Get it *all* out, all those concepts. Explore how to best do so. We all have different ways of working. Find the way that's right for you.

Here are a few tips to try:

- Write everything on a whiteboard

- Sit with a friend; say it all, record it

- Talk into your smart phone

- Type it into a document

- Take a pad of paper and start writing

Personally, I like to sit with a piece of paper and just go crazy. Or sometimes, I use a whiteboard. I fill up one side, flip it over, and fill up the other. The objective is to get all the concepts floating around in my head into some physical form. This brings clarity.

What you now have are pieces of a puzzle. Move them around. This fits here, that fits there. That piece over there? You're not quite sure yet where it fits, but you sense that it fits somewhere. Put it aside; save it for later.

Now focus on what's most immediately relevant. Commence to tinkering. Tweak it, refine it, hone it down to its essence.

There may be multiple methods of getting it all out there that work well for you. Investigate. Explore. Try out a few. I sometimes use a combination. There's no right way, no one-size-fits-all approach.

(Here's another tip: Take advantage of quiet time in your car to gather your thoughts. Appreciate it. Take advantage of it, to generate ideas. Talk into your phone. I used to be afraid of silence. Now, I very often crave it—a respite from all the noise.)

No matter what medium you opt for, forget about form, sentence structure, complete sentences, fully formed thoughts, etc. Don't even worry yet about it all making good sense.

And please don't focus on *narrowing* the messaging. Go broad. Get it all out there, even things that might seem (at present) silly or irrelevant. It popped into your head—maybe there's a good reason, one that just hasn't yet revealed itself. Just capture it all.

Once it's all out there, it's time to begin the process of crafting that simple, persuasive message. This content will be a living message; it'll continue to evolve over time. Don't aim for perfection. Your goal is to refine and improve the messaging as you walk through these steps.

Z. ASK YOURSELF: "WHAT PROBLEM DOES THIS SOLVE?"

Every human being has three fundamental areas of concern: money, relationships, and health. Despite life's complexities, most all problems can be tossed into one of these buckets. Offering solutions to issues in one of those categories is a great way to motivate people to take action.

The common practice in marketing a product or service is to stress its selling points. But that might not be exactly the right motivation. If you want people to care, show them how what you're offering will solve a real problem they face.

Start with the problem/solution model: My audience has a problem, and I can solve it. If nothing immediately stands out, this would be a great time to reread all your content and identify the problems you can potentially solve. People will pay attention if you're solving a real problem for them.

I regularly use an app called SendJim. It's a service that sends out hand-written notes, has gifts delivered—it does all kinds of things I have difficulty finding time to do on my own. I understand the value of the extra gesture, of a personalized service. But I'm a businessman and a dad, and I generally just don't have the time to do all that on my own. So I'm willing to pay a surcharge for it.

My monthly razor service is another example. It saves me time. It solves a problem.

So what are you bringing to people that they're willing to pay you for? That's what you need to focus on, not on all the bells and whistles and all the wonderful things your product or service can deliver—at least not yet. No. First, you need to articulate what problem you've arrived to solve.

So, can you, in one succinct sentence, explain what that is?

Look at these two sentences. What's different about them?

My new book, Pixels Are the New Ink, *gives advice for building your social profiles.*

My new book, Pixels Are the New Ink, *teaches thought leaders like you how to make money sharing information already in your head—online.*

While the first sentence is true, it isn't persuasive. The second sentence, on the other hand, assumes that my reader would like to make more money (and that's probably a fair assumption of most people) and offers the opportunity to do so.

Do you think I have their attention? Likely so.

Time to move on to the next step.

3. ASK WHAT IS CRUCIAL. STRIKE EVERYTHING ELSE.

৹ ৹ ৹

"The ability to simplify means to eliminate the unnecessary so the necessary may speak."

—Hans Hoffman—

৹ ৹ ৹

I vividly remember the first paper I submitted in graduate school. I was rather proud of it, actually. I put a lot of thought and work into that paper. I was quite certain it was the best in the class.

But my English professor didn't see my work in exactly the same light. My masterpiece was returned to me, bleeding a slow death of red ink, with a note asking me to speak with her.

How could this be? My undergraduate English professors loved my work. Though they consistently offered ways to improve, they never totally rejected my writing. But, in this case, I was called out for verbosity. In my quest to appear smart, I'd loaded every paragraph with every concept within the universe. And, as a result, I'd failed. Miserably.

I'd like to say that my "masterpiece" just needed some slight revisions. But, in reality, it needed total reconstruction. My writing needed to be reborn.

I'm convinced that, as you've started drafting your thoughts, you're a lot closer to your intent than I was with my first grad school paper. But there's likely some bloat. As you craft your message, read with a critical eye. You'll likely immediately begin to see what needs to be trimmed. Focus on eliminating any and all unnecessary elements.

Let's go ahead and get this out there now: Most likely, your users won't care as much as you do. So give them only what's necessary.

One of the greatest lessons Twitter has taught me is how to reduce content and communicate only what's most important. Maybe you've done this, too: You type out your tweet, and it's 180 characters long. You then begin to remove unnecessary words, even letters, until you hit that magical 140.

This is the same process I'm advocating for here, just on a larger scale. Take out your red pen. Start striking through non-crucial elements. Ask yourself what details really don't matter. Everything else must go!

But what I mean by that is that it must go for now. Just for now. There's probably value in that content, just not quite yet—not here in the core. Don't discard it, just file it away for now. There may well be some very important points in there that will come in handy later.

Think in terms of creating an inverted funnel of information, and share that information in stages. For example, if your messaging lives in an online petition, you can capture email addresses as people sign it. If they allow you to keep the communication alive via email, you can develop a campaign that feeds them this additional information. You can take a similar approach if you're communicating about a product you're selling.

Prior to Twitter, most of us didn't appreciate the value of shorter messages. But shorter is where we've arrived. Facebook is now prompting you to write more succinct messages. They know people will respond better, and so they'll put it in a bigger font.

So ask yourself: What does this word add? If it adds nothing, lose it. Take it to the extreme: Can you convey everything you want to say in a single word? If so, do so. It's more likely that your reader will stick around.

This is all about honing your message, then broadening it as your opportunities unfold. There will soon be opportunities to delve deeper. But start off too deep, and you're going to lose your audience. Save that more penetrating material. You'll need it later.

Think one word at a time. People are making decisions one word at a time. Too many details, too much embellishment too soon—they're gone.

And the final step . . .

4. REMOVE ALL INTERNAL (OR GENERALLY UNKNOWN) JARGON

We often communicate with insider language that isolates those who aren't "in the know." Perhaps it makes us feel smarter—a member of some inner circle—to use esoteric terms. But anytime there's an inner circle, there are, by definition, people left outside.

There's a fine line between conveying that you're the expert and using "insider-y" language. Old-school thinking was that, when you pitch, you want to wow them with the jargon. Those days are gone.

Be careful not to unnecessarily alienate the people you're actually trying to persuade. If the internal jargon isn't necessary, strike it. If you use an acronym, define it. Then stick with it.

Here's an example of what can go wrong when you use an unnecessary acronym:

While writing copy, you use an obscure, undefined acronym. Your user Googles it to learn its meaning. Another person, vying for your user's attention, serves up an interesting ad on that page. Your user clicks that ad, which is actually an action-packed video. While watching the video, a text message pops up. It's an invite to dinner. Think your user cares about your message now? Probably not. Now the question is, "What's for dinner?"

Bottom line: Don't create barriers with language. When it's time to introduce denser language, introduce it with some context.

"Simplicity is an exact medium between too little and too much." – Sir Joshua Reynolds

Here's what we learned: Less is more. Focus only on what is necessary and important. Everything can be saved for later.

Another industry expert's perspective:

> Early in my writing career, I learned to ask *"so what"* after each sentence written, to make sure that each word had a purpose, and offered value to the message and the reader. Whether it was a blog post or leadership tip that I've circulated monthly since 2004, I've been carefully aware of the mission of getting people hooked immediately, or risk losing them forever. I do that by putting my head into their shoes (that's just thinking about what it's like to be them), and serving up what they want immediately. We could ramble on our keyboards typing so much content, but the real nugget that people can expect to take away and keep for a long time is just a tiny little bite sized habit breaking, new

habit-forming idea, phrase or story. Here's how I "so what" my writing after it's drafted, to make sure it catches the audience's attention.

> Example: One of the root causes of conflict that I've experienced while working with many organizations is that front line leaders—supervisors promoted from the front line level—don't often have the skills necessary to manage people. *So What?*
>
> Some tend to say the wrong thing, or say things the wrong way, or handle issues and problems less effectively than they could. *So What?*
>
> Conflict is a high cost that is quite preventable. *So What?*

Solution = Training.

By reviewing my work, I ask, "So What?" at the same time I imagine myself in the audience asking that question to evaluate whether that sentence gives me something of value, or if its just a bunch of hot air.

People want WIIFM . . . (what's in it for me? . . . so just give it to them)

—Penny Tremblay
PennyTremblay.com

Ready for the next step? Let's talk about how to capture your audience's attention early.

Questions for Reflection

1. Think through some area in which you need to persuade. Take a few minutes to debrief yourself. What is the simple essence of what you want to communicate? Can you say it in 25 words or less?

2. What problem does this solve for the person you're trying to persuade?

3. Reread your response to #1. Have you framed this concept from your audience's need or your own?

4. Reread your response to #1. Are there any words you can strike? Look critically at each word.

5. Now, can you communicate the main message in #1 in 10 words or less?

Chapter 4

CAPTURING THEIR ATTENTION EARLY

"Sometimes a scream is better than a thesis."
—Ralph Waldo Emerson —

Perhaps more than ever before, you're going to have to work hard to capture your audience's attention. Some studies indicate that our attention span today is less than that of a goldfish. Whether in person, on the phone, or online, you've got but seconds to capture your audience's attention.

A study from Canada illustrates this point. It concluded that attention spans have decreased from twelve seconds to eight seconds since the mobile revolution began in 2010. And content is being consumed on mobile devices now more than ever.

People today have a lot of noise thrown at them; they're bombarded almost every waking moment. The Internet has made content generation so easy, which is great; it's an accessible platform on which to communicate.

On the other hand, the fact that it's so easy means anybody can post things. There's so much out there. Just think about what an average Google search yields. Finding what's most relevant takes some digging and a discerning mind.

As I noted earlier, readers today more commonly scan than read. They're making decisions in two to three seconds on whether to stay on a page or exit. That's why those first couple of sentences are so critical. The goal is to immediately pique interest. How do I capture their attention sufficiently enough that they're ready to move forward with me—to give up the time when time is so constrained? They're not going to read sentence three if they're not engaged with the first two.

If you're failing to cut through the clamor, your readers will tell you really fast, by not responding.

I do a lot of research to see what resonates online. I use Twitter to test messaging. It's very easy to create 140 characters and try out several versions of a message, to determine which one gets clicked, retweeted, liked. You should do whatever testing you can early on.

I grew up respecting the "golden rule." You know, "Do unto others as you would have them do unto you." Then once I entered the business world, the rule changed to, "The one with the gold rules." But in today's digital world, it's shifted again. Today, we say, "The thumb rules."

What does this mean? Watch someone on their phone. The thumb scrolls feverishly, wending its way through content as it sits on its throne of decision-making. People are making decisions with the thumb; sometimes, the thumb moves ahead of the brain. This tendency isn't generational, as some argue. Young people may have shorter attention spans, but I go out to dinner with people in their fifties and sixties who can't stop looking at their phones.

Every link clicked must pass the thumb test, and most links fail. You have two seconds to keep the thumb from moving on. What makes your content any more likely to be clicked?

If you want your content to be consumed, you must win over the thumb. Your audience has a world of choices, with access to more content than could ever be consumed.

But here's a secret: Most content is vanilla, boring, mundane, unexciting, monotonous, ordinary, uninteresting . . . It doesn't take a whole lot to stand out; the bar isn't that high. You can prevail.

In most cases, you'll have primary, secondary, and tertiary goals for your messaging. When I'm trying to close a deal with a client, whether online or otherwise, I aim to operate in three steps: know, like, trust. These steps need to be well defined up front. And they have to be done in order—no jumping around.

Again: know, like, trust.

Your audience must first come to know you. They can't make a decision to move forward with you if they don't know who you are. In that first step, your goal may simply be brand awareness—you simply want them to learn your name. You craft messaging, share on social media, people see your name and, perhaps, form some type of impression.

But if you need action—like signing a petition—and they don't click through, you're not succeeding. *You only have seconds to capture their attention.* You must immediately stand out.

ᴑ ᴑ ᴑ

"Writers have nanoseconds to compel readers before they flit to another headline or toast another Pop Tart."
—David A. Fryxell—

ᴑ ᴑ ᴑ

If they didn't click through, does that mean they don't like you? Not necessarily. It could be any number of things. Maybe their kids started screaming. Maybe the phone rang. A text message popped up. They abandoned you (for the moment). Don't take it personally. Don't give up. Analyze it to the extent that you can. Maybe something's just a bit off. Examine it, but don't beat yourself up. Strive to improve.

The beauty of online content is its immediacy; we're constantly getting feedback. You run a direct-mail campaign, and once you've printed it out and sent it off, it's done. But, online, when people aren't responding, you can immediately make adjustments.

Your readers are informing you. Listen. Learn what you can through trial and error. And be willing to accept it without internalizing. This just didn't work. Okay. What does work?

A word of caution:

You want to stand out in a way that matches who you are; all communication should stay true to your established brand. Otherwise, you send mixed messaging, giving the user whiplash.

Be unique, stand out, give the thumb a reason to click—but stay true to your brand messaging. When we represent our brand in such a way that deviates from who we are, it works against us. People need to see the consistency of a brand over and over.

I know from personal experience the cost of ill-advised brand deviation. Once, in an attempt to grab attention, I deviated from my personal brand standards. I wanted to try something new. There are people online who have a very snarky voice; they can get away with it because that's who they are; that's the brand they've established.

But that's not who I am; that's not my brand. Mine is much more colloquial, friendlier. That's what I try to convey. Not snark. And when I tried it in a blog post, it backfired; it blew up. It was horrible. And it took time to repair. It just wasn't who I was, and it made my audience angry. To those people I'd offended, I apologized, privately. And, in my public profile, I went back to who I am.

It's okay to push your brand, but you need to understand where the boundaries are. If you need six or seven interactions, they can't be all over the place, lest people become confused about what your brand represents.

Okay, so you've got your basic messaging in hand. Now, run it through the following filters. Use these eight tips to help you craft messaging that will capture attention:

1. START WITH THEM

Find a way to use the word "you" at least once. Do this very early. By speaking to your audience directly, using the word "you," you'll pull users into your messaging and allow them to feel a connection: "Let's talk." You're identifying with them. Can you show you understand their struggles, fears, frustrations? If so, you'll connect early on in your messaging, increasing the likelihood they'll continue to listen to you.

2. USE SHORT SENTENCES

Your freshman English professor will probably balk at this statement. Most of them taught us to write sophisticated sentences, with modifiers and connectors and whatnot. But, online, you need to use short, powerful sentences. Push for the period sooner than later. Why? As stated earlier, people don't read, they scan.

Why use truncated sentences? Because they . . .

- boil things down to their essence
- create a sense of urgency or tension
- provide immediate emphasis on the power words (single words that convey a mental picture; the association is immediately there).

George Orwell's *1984* has recently popped back into public discourse. If you aren't familiar with it, the novel is about a man who fights the totalitarian power of government (i.e. Big Brother).

The book begins with a short, powerful sentence: "He loved Big Brother." A longer, complex sentence wouldn't have packed the punch that this simple, four-word sentence does.

Don't be afraid to use short sentences. They're crucial to your success in persuading others.

Do you know the shortest sentence in the English version of the Bible? It's only two words: "Jesus wept." That sentence packs in so many emotions: this all-powerful persona, God, is humanized. That a god would weep? That pulls me in. Tell me that Jesus wept, and I can start filling in the rest. I connect better than I would with the details. That's why it works.

If you want to master the short sentence, check out Verlyn Klinkenborg's book *Several Short Sentences About Writing*. Or read a lot of Hemmingway.

If writing shorter sentences doesn't put your freshman comp teacher into conniptions, this technique definitely will: Use only phrases, or even single words. Seriously.

Want a powerful way to create a linguistic zinger? Use a phrase as a sentence. The gods of writing won't put a curse on you. There will be no voodoo doll with pins in it. I promise. Rather, your readers will instantly feel and understand what you're trying to convey.

And here's another tip: Repeat a short sentence. That's right. Say it again. Your copy will be burned into your reader's brain. Say it again.

3. ASK YOUR READER A QUESTION

Encourage your readers to pause, even slightly, and think. And if they're thinking, they're engaged. Try asking a question early on. It gets your users to pause and think. Any successful attempts to get them to slow down will likely keep them engaged into the next sentence.

4. USE A SHOCKING QUOTE

Howard Stern is often referred to as a shock jock, a reference to his willingness to say shocking things in his role as a radio host. He has a willingness to say just about anything about anyone—including the Pope.

Here's what he said: "I'm sickened by all religions. Religion has divided people. I don't think there's any difference between the Pope wearing a large hat and parading around with a smoking purse and an African painting his face while praying to a rock."

If you're anything like me, that statement caught your attention. And likely, his quote has evoked some type of emotion in you. A shocking quote can definitely arouse curiosity, but it has to have meaning and relevance to both the audience and the subject matter.

A shocking quote has the potential to capture attention or evoke emotion. And if you're really successful, it'll do both.

5. SHARE A STATISTIC

Toss out a mind-blowing statistic. For example, say you're trying to persuade a potential client that email marketing is still effective. Try a statistic like this: Gmail alone has one billion users, and it is expected to grow beyond three billion users by 2020.

6. SHARE A FACT

By definition, a fact is true. Sharing a fact makes you seem more credible. Just make sure the fact is powerful, relevant, and interesting. And factual. Sharing a fact may well also cause your reader to pause and ponder, and that's a good thing.

Sharing a fact is especially helpful when you're trying to persuade outside your area of expertise. Quote someone who's an expert. How many times have you heard a statement like, "Four out of five dentists recommend . . .?" If that many dentists say it's true, it must be true, right?

7. INVITE YOUR READER TO IMAGINE

Using the word "imagine" helps your audience form a mental picture of something that's not present. And it also frees the mind to accept this reality with little evidence. You're encouraging them to picture the situation in the way you want them to see it. This technique works because you set them free from the current circumstances and allow them to imagine an entirely different situation. And this different situation is the one you believe will move them.

Back during the 2016 presidential election, you might have heard something like this: "Imagine life under President Hillary Clinton. Your Second Amendment rights taken away forever. Donating to the NRA has never been more important."

Do you think this content would capture the attention of gun-rights activists and have them pulling out their credit cards? For sure. And, in this example, the use of "imagine" is even more powerful because it's coupled with loss aversion, something we'll discuss in Chapter 8.

8. DISRUPT YOUR AUDIENCE

Most of us are creatures of habit. We take the familiar, comfortable path. Want to capture someone's attention very quickly? Break this path of comfort. Say something that disrupts normal expectations.

You have limited time to capture users' attention, so every word must be crafted with purpose and care. Experiment with some of these techniques to quickly capture your readers attention. David Murray pointedly asks this question that applies to your ability to capture users' attention early: "If nobody hears your strategic messaging, does it make a sound?

Ready for the next step? Let's talk about how to craft a sticky message.

Questions for Reflection

1. What ways of capturing attention early have worked for you in the past?

2. What techniques for capturing attention would you like to try? Do they align with your brand?

3. At the end of Chapter 3, you crafted a simple message. How can you support that message in a way that captures attention? Which of the techniques in this chapter do you think will work best?

4. Rewrite your simple message and add in techniques to capture attention.

5. Test this on a potential audience to determine if your techniques worked. If not, try a different approach.

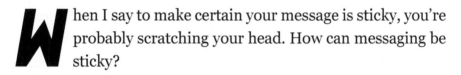

MAKING IT STICKY

"If they can't repeat it, they didn't get it."

—Sam Horn —

When I say to make certain your message is sticky, you're probably scratching your head. How can messaging be sticky?

Have you ever stepped in gum? Of course. We've all been there. You're walking along, and all of a sudden, there's a slight drag on your shoe—not enough to stop you in your tracks, but definitely enough to notice. And, if you continue walking, you'll sense the traction of this gum sticking to your shoe.

This is an analogy for what I mean when I say you need to craft a sticky message.

Consider this from Wilhelm Schnotz:

> Americans are exposed to hundreds of advertisements, marketing efforts and websites each day. How many of those do people actually remember a few hours later? Marketers and advertising professionals refer to memorable ad campaigns as "sticky," because they stick with audiences long after

they've been exposed to them, and Web marketing gurus refer to websites that make visitors want to stick around instead of surfing as "sticky." Developing sticky marketing requires a different approach than many advertisers take when developing their strategy.

Each day, we're bombarded with messages, and our ability to absorb them—our bandwidth—is limited. Most of that messaging just slips away, as if off Teflon. You must find a way to make your messaging resonate. You must make it stick.

Stickiness matters for two primary reasons:

First, you want your message to remain top of mind. Something needs to trigger in the brain to keep your information front and center. And secondly, since it will likely take multiple times of your intended audience seeing your messaging before they'll take action, you want people to remember this initial messaging so that making the connection with future ones will likely be more easily retrievable.

Generally speaking, people will need exposure to your content six or seven times before moving from awareness to action. And you'll want to make sure they can see the connection with each new view.

In his book *The Respect Effect,* Paul Meshanko describes a successful ad campaign in order to explain why reposting is so important: "No matter how compelling the message, if it's played only once or twice, there's very little chance of it influencing perceptions and intentions strongly enough to result in the desired buyer behaviors."

Brands understand the importance of saying the same thing over and over. You may feel like it's redundant and boring. But your audience needs the repetition. Check out this list of time-tested slogans Jeffry Pilcher pulled together. I'm willing to bet you'll agree that well over half of these are "sticky":

Got milk?
(used for 21 years, starting in 1993)

Just do it.
(used for more than 26 years, starting in 1988)

What happens here, stays here.
(used for more than 15 years, starting in 2003)

Tastes great, less filling.
(used since the 1970s)

Good to the last drop.
(used for more than 97 years, starting in 1917)

Melts in your mouth, not in your hands.
(used for more than 60 years, since 1954)

Breakfast of Champions.
(used for more than 87 years, starting in 1927)

Plop, plop, fizz, fizz, oh what a relief it is.
(used for more than 43 years, starting in 1971)

Creating sticky messaging isn't an elusive task. There are concrete devices you can use to make sure your messaging remains with your users. Here are a few to get you started:

REPETITION

This device is pretty obvious: Repeat the same words within your core messaging. You can make a single word or multiple words much more impactful when you help your audience focus on what's most important.

There are more ways to structure repetition than you probably realize. It can be more sophisticated than just repeating the same word multiple times. Consider these variations on repetition:

- **Anadiplosis:** Repetition of the last word in a line or clause

- **Anaphora:** Repetition of words at the start of clauses or verses

- **Antistasis:** Repetition of words or phrases in opposite sense

- **Diacope:** Repetition of words broken by other words

- **Epanalepsis:** Repetition of the same words at the end and start of a sentence

- **Epimone:** Repetition of a phrase (usually a question) to stress a point

- **Epiphora:** Repetition of the same word at the end of each clause

- **Gradatio:** A construction in poetry where the last word of one clause becomes the first of the next, and so on

- **Negative-Positive Restatement:** Repetition of an idea first in negative terms and then in positive terms

- **Polyptoton:** Repetition of words of the same root with different endings

- **Symploce:** A combination of anaphora and epiphora in which repetition is both at the end and the beginning

Take a look at this literary example of epiphora from Shusaku Endo in his novel *Deep River*:

"Hatred was spreading everywhere, blood was being spilled everywhere, wars were breaking out everywhere."

The word "everywhere" sticks, right? It's especially effective at the end of the phrases because the punctuation creates a natural pause.

Or how about this example from Ann Patchett's *The Patron Saint of Liars*. Notable in this instance is the repetition of a phrase: "So I said yes to Thomas Clinton and later thought that I had said yes to God and later still realized I had said yes only to Thomas Clinton."

Are you ready to say "yes?" I sure am!

If there's a single word or short phrase that's important to your messaging, then consider using repetition. The frequency of use will give the word power, make it stick with your audience, and help drive home your point.

ALLITERATION

Alliteration is the occurrence of the same letter or sound at the beginning of adjacent or closely connected words—such as the two "M"s in Moonlight Madness. It signals to the reader that the words are important. It also often makes the words fun to repeat.

If you've paid any attention to national politics in the past few years, you've probably heard this short phrase: "Repeal and Replace."

It's been everywhere, right? House Speaker Paul Ryan once suggested that every Congressional Republican runs on repealing and replacing the Affordable Care Act. Audiences typically respond instantly and passionately. Why does it work? One reason is the use of alliteration in those action verbs makes this a strong, memorable phrase. It's solid.

RHYMING

For those of you who love order and symmetry, this device will likely make your list. Rhyming gives structure, often cadence, and definitely helps people remember the message. This section on rhyming is not designed to be exhaustive. There are textbooks that go deep into the various forms of rhyming. Rather, I want to offer a few options that could easily be implemented into your sticky messaging.

I grew up on nursery rhymes; I think we all did. This particular rhyme is probably the most familiar in the English language:

Humpty Dumpty sat on a wall,

Humpty Dumpty had a great fall.

All the king's horses and all the king's men . . .

Can you say the final line? Of course, you can. In fact, you probably can't restrain yourself from saying, "Couldn't put Humpty together again."

Or how about this tagline? Heard it? "Bounty—the quicker picker-upper."

I don't think I can even say "Bounty" without adding that tag. Are you the same?

Rhyming copy will help your message stick. And there are so many forms of rhymes that you can find what really works for you and perhaps add a bit of nuanced sophistication. Take a look at these variations and options:

Perfect rhyme
Perhaps the most well-known of all types of rhyme, the perfect rhyme is:

- exemplified by homonyms, such as bear/bare or wear/where;

- one in which different consonants are followed by identical vowel and consonant sounds, such as in moon and June.

General types of rhyme

The term "general rhyme" refers to a variety of phonetic like-nesses between words. Here are four examples:

- Syllabic rhymes: Syllabic rhymes are words in which the last syllables sound similar but without a stressed vowel. Examples are bottle/fiddle, cleaver/silver, pitter/patter.

- Assonance: Assonance rhymes (also known as slant rhymes) are words that have the same vowel sound—like slow/road and shake/mate—and can be placed in such phrases as, "Try as I might, the kite did not fly."

- Imperfect rhymes: Imperfect rhymes are rhymes where either the vowels or the consonants of the stressed syllables are the same. They can also be referred to as off rhymes, oblique rhymes, near rhymes, and half rhymes. Some examples are moon/run, hold/bald, eyes/light, years/yours.

- Eye rhymes: Although I don't recommend using eye rhymes, I do want to bring them to your attention. Also called sight or spelling rhymes, this type of rhyming has words that "look" like they rhyme but are pronounced differently. These are words like food/flood, cough/bough, laughter/slaughter, love/move. . . I think you get the picture. I don't prefer these in copy because they don't ring out. And our goal here is to be memorable and stick.

Often, there's a bonus to rhyming: cadence. Cadence is derived from the Latin word *cadentia*, which means "a falling." Linguists refer to this as the prosodic pattern. Check out this example from a recent political activist's sign:

Can't build a wall.
Hands too small.

Know what this sign is referencing? Know who it is referencing? I bet so. And what a catchy phrase, the epitome of a sticky message.

Again, your goal is to make sure your messaging sticks to your reader as part of the process of moving them to responding to your call to action. I encourage you to try several of these techniques. Find what works for you and your message. Get out of your comfort zone a bit. Have some fun, and craft a message that will last.

You now have plenty of creative ways to make your messaging sticky. Which leads us to one final question: How do you determine which words to select? Which words should you repeat?

Although there are numerous ways to approach this question, perhaps the simplest way is to ask yourself which words . . .

- Are most important?
- Help to emphasize your main point?
- Help to make an emotional connection?
- Connect with an already known/experienced fact?

Ready for the next step? Let's talk about how to help others find their win.

Questions for Reflection

1. What sticky messages come to your mind?

2. What characteristics of those messages cause them to remain in your memory?

3. Look back at the simple message you crafted in Chapter 3 and the techniques in this chapter. How can you write your message in such a way that it remains top of mind for others?

4. Try a different approach. Rewrite your message using a different technique for making it sticky.

5. Sometimes, in trying to create a cute, sticky message, we break from our brand standards. Reviewing your sticky messages, do they stay true to the brand you're creating?

Chapter 6

HELPING OTHERS FIND THEIR WIN

"You will get everything in life that you want if you just help enough other people get what they want."

—Zig Ziglar—

*T*he challenge was daunting, but achievable. It was consequential and had the potential to create a lot of money. And although critics said it could never happen, I believed it could.

I'm talking about a grassroots campaign I led: The North Carolina Brunch Bill. The state's Blue laws prohibited restaurants and other venues from selling alcohol before noon on Sundays. The rationale was that we had to protect the church, and Sunday church service ended at noon. So before noon, no alcohol. After noon, go for it.

I was hired by a national organization to build a grassroots coalition to support the lobbyists for the restaurant industry and a statewide association as they carefully, and with precision, navigated the North Carolina General Assembly.

Our slogan was "Free the Mimosa." My objective was to give people what they wanted, and what they wanted was the occasional mimosa before noon on a Sunday.

In the end, I built the largest grassroots program for a state campaign that my client had ever seen. One of our call-to-action drives generated more email responses than my client had ever received on any campaign. But, more importantly, I helped navigate the bill through the state Senate and House of Representatives by motivating citizens across the state to take action when I needed it.

Here's what I knew: This wasn't about my client passing a bill. This was about citizens across the state who had likely tried to order a Sunday morning mimosa, only to be told no. They wanted a drink with brunch on Sundays. So that's where I focused.

Let's be honest, most of us strategize to find ways to win. Obviously, given that you're reading this book, you do, too. And more often than not, we're thinking about winning from our own perspective. But, to be successful, you have to be where your audience is. You have to make it about them.

I recently received the following email, and I think it's a good example of the opposite of what I've described above:

> Jeff,
>
> We're really trying to fill the room on this one. We've got some congressional staff that will be in attendance and some higher-ups from DC in town.
>
> Do you think you can help us get some attendees?
>
> Thanks!
> Xxxxxx

Although I like the sender as a person, I had no motivation to jump in. I was swamped with my own to-do list, emails to return, writing, etc. Like always, I faced a day with lots of problems to solve. Could I have helped? Did I know people I could have urged to attend this event? Did I have the ability to reach out to them? Yes. But I didn't. The sender didn't persuade me. The request was about him, what he needed, with no attempt to convince me that attending would be good for me, as well.

But with a few quick tweaks to the ask, I might have responded differently. Take a look at this revised version:

> Jeff,
>
> We've got some congressional staff that will be in attendance and some higher-ups from DC in town, and I know you are building your network of DC power players. The room is full, but I could add you and a couple friends if you want to bring someone.
>
> Thanks!
> Xxxxxx

Do you see the difference? I can tell you that I likely would have responded to the revised version. That version is written in a way that shows me how the request meets my needs. And the sender would have won, too.

We often think of persuasion as a way to get what we want. We want to get elected. We want a bill passed. Or we want to close a big deal. Maybe it's an employer making a job offer.

Regardless of the "thing," our mission is clear: We want to win, and we know this often means persuading others to embrace our perspective.

It's all about your audience. Always. They care about themselves, their health, finances, and families and friends. Your challenge is to remove yourself, to begin to see things through your audience's perspective, and to find a way to message from their needs, wants, and desires. Step into their shoes. What matters to them? Determine what that is, and adjust your messaging accordingly. Speak to their needs. Address those needs, and you'll win, as well.

So, how do you help others find their win? I think it can be broken down into three easy steps: listening to where your audience is, asking questions, and then seeking alignment. Let's walk through three effective tools to make your audience your primary focus.

1. FIRST, LISTEN.

You have a lot to say. I get that. We all do. And I'm willing to bet you're passionate about the issue at hand. That's fantastic. But are you willing to put that on the back burner—just for the moment—to listen? There's information you need, and you'll only get it by listening.

Too often, when we have a point to make, or we want to persuade someone, we go right at them—"you need this, this, and this"—rather than starting with a question. What do they need? Why do they need it?

Too often, we go in attempting to bang people over the head with *our* point of view. And very often, people feel as if no one is interested in *their* point of view. They want someone to listen—to try to understand their point of view. Try to understand their perspective, where they're coming from. Effectively reaching people is a matter of understanding where they're coming from and attempting to respond to their needs.

It's important to remember that hearing and listening are not the same thing. Hearing is involuntary; listening is going to require effort.

We're talking here about three types of listening: (1) informational listening (to learn); (2) critical listening (to evaluate); and (3) therapeutic or empathetic listening (to understand feelings).

I suggest you prepare to listen by making sure you have an open, nonjudgmental mindset. At this stage—the introductory stage—it's important to remember there's nothing to fix; this isn't about solutions. Author and educator Stephen R. Covey once said, "Many people do not listen with the intent to understand; they listen with the intent to reply."

Make sure you're actively listening. Turn your phone off. Often, instead of listening, we start forming thoughts, responses, arguments, etc. None of these matter in the introductory stage. All that matters is that you're in the moment and truly *listening*.

What the person says is important, but so is what is not said. To quote the late Peter Drucker, a management consultant and author, "The most important thing in communication is hearing what isn't said." Body language, facial expressions, and words left out can be clues. Recognize when you're treading on uncertain terrain. Backup; assess.

For most people, being an active listener isn't natural; it takes practice. Seek to understand, not to be understood. What is their need? Can you meet it? Your win is the fulfillment of their needs.

Here's what I can promise you: If you'll commit to active listening, people will tell you everything you need to know.

2. NEXT, ASK QUESTIONS.

One of the best ways to show you're listening, while also showing that you value what your audience is saying, is to ask questions. Allow your audience to communicate without being judged.

I would encourage you to refrain from leading questions. At this stage, it isn't about taking your audience somewhere. It's really about understanding them.

Ask open-ended questions; they encourage your audience to elaborate, offer more developed thoughts. Simple "yes" or "no" questions aren't likely to give you the depth you need. Open-ended questions encourage your audience to offer greater detail: "Why, how, what do you think about . . ."

Examples of clarifying questions that can elicit a more detailed response are, "Did I hear you say . . ." or, "Can you explain more about . . ."

Also, try asking questions that might uncover emotions. "How does this make you feel?" "What I heard you say is . . ."

How do you make sure you're actually listening and understanding correctly? Repeat back to them their words to make certain you heard what they're actually saying.

3. FINALLY, SEEK ALIGNMENT.

Here's where your magic begins to happen. This is the phase where your skills really come into play.

You understand exactly where you want your audience to be. You understand where they are. You understand why they are where they are. You understand your message and reason for persuasion. Now, the question is, "Where is the alignment?"

Let me give you a good example of following the three steps I've just introduced.

I recently heard about a guy running for city council in a city near where I live. He launched his campaign by walking around, going door to door, getting to know people, and asking them, "What's going on in your neighborhood?" "What are your concerns?" "What can I do to help you?" Several people mentioned an intersection at which there was a high rate of accidents.

So he went there and parked his car near the intersection. And, after observing for a few hours, he saw that only about one in ten motorists were correctly following the traffic signs. Were the signs poorly positioned? Or too vague? Or did more awareness need to be raised about the potential danger? It was an issue he needed to further explore.

He'd listened, asked questions, learned, then followed up on his constituents' concern. My guess is that he's got a good crack at getting elected. He's aligned with those constituents.

Now, can you move *your* audience? Can you solve their problem and demonstrate the value? Can you understand them and guide them to a new place? Frame your conversation by speaking to the values of the people you wish to persuade.

Again, winning is ultimately about your audience. Help them find success, and *you'll* find success. You can persuade them. You can get what you want. Just start with them. Help *them* win, and *you'll win*, too.

Another industry expert's perspective:

> Life with three children presents distinct challenges when pizza is involved. You know what I mean, right? Each sibling watches the other take a piece of the pie and that means one less for them, and as they watch the pizza slowly disappear, desperation sets in and fighting ensues in order for every kid to get as much as they want.
>
> Pizza is a zero-sum game—meaning that, when someone takes a piece, that is one less piece for them.
>
> As leaders and influencers, we have this tendency to see

life like a pizza—that, when someone gets accolades or the promotion or opportunities, that means less for us. And this mentality creates competition and fear—it creates a dog-eat-dog environment that diminishes us all.

You know what I mean. Think of a recent interaction you had with a co-worker or manager that put you down, that diminished your talents, or dismissed your accomplishments. How did that make you feel? Probably pretty lousy. These types of leaders are like vampires—sucking the life out of everyone else in order for them to survive. And be careful—their negativity can be contagious, creating a toxic culture of that leaves everyone hurt.

Now, think of the last time someone listened to you attentively, saw your gifts and talents, encouraged you to be your best, and went out of their way to help you succeed—even when it was inconvenient for them, or even if they had to sacrifice for you. How did that make you feel? Probably pretty great. And now, if they needed help, would you help them? Yes! Of course!

This is win-win leadership. Where leaders see the gifts of those around them and empower everyone to live their best lives—to succeed—even if it means they leave the company to take a promotion or need to take time off to attend to a personal dream. I call these people "compassionate influencers." These influencers do not see the world like pizza—but are confident and secure enough to see there's enough success to go around, and that, by helping others succeed, they will succeed, too. As the old saying goes, "A rising tide raises all boats."

We are at our best when we are functioning in compassion. Science is proving that, when functioning in compassion, we are actually healthier, happier, and our relationships thrive. Helping others get their "win" releases oxytocin throughout our bodies which propels our minds, connects us to others, and eases our stress. Helping others get their "win" eliminates the barriers of competition, opens up opportunities for collaboration and partnership, and lays the foundation for a culture of success for everyone involved.

Life doesn't have to be a zero-sum game where some "win" and others "lose." We live in a world of abundance where there is room for everyone to thrive and live their best lives. I believe it's these compassionate leaders who empower those around them to reach their dreams that build loyalty and create a culture of success where everyone's ship rises together. We can choose to live in a win-win world!

Jason Butler
JasonPButler.com

Ready for the next step? Let's talk about how to make a connection.

Questions for Reflection

1. How can you check your motives, and your heart, to understand whether or not you're really focusing on others?

2. How do you know if you're truly valuing the input and needs of others, or merely going through the motions to get what you want?

3. Think back to moments in which you know your focus was on others. How did that person respond?

4. Where do you think the boundary lies in making sure you focus on others while remaining cognizant of taking care of yourself?

5. Look back at the message you created in the reflection section of Chapter 3. Does it focus on the win of your audience? If not, how can you rewrite it to put the focus on them?

Chapter 7

MAKING A CONNECTION

"A dream you dream alone is only a dream. A dream you dream together is reality."

—John Lennon—

People who are able to persuade often have one key trait in common: They know how to connect. I believe that, at its core, persuasion is a conversation. And the best conversations involve a connection.

We've all sat through presentations where the keynote speaker fails to connect. It feels like a struggle. Checking email on our phones seems more rewarding than listening to a speaker who seems to be way off in the distance.

Connecting matters. In fact, I'd argue that a connection is necessary for persuasion.

Ever listened to a speaker, lost all awareness of time, felt like it was just you and the speaker, and every word seemed to resonate within you? That's what I mean by connection. Show me any great person able to persuade, and I'll bet we can find where she was able to connect with her audience.

I'm about to show you several powerful techniques that will serve you well as you make a connection with your audience. But perhaps this one objective tops them all: Strive to understand.

I think a willingness to understand where others are at in their lives is lacking in our society. People often focus on why the other viewpoint is wrong, and often even demonize their audience because of this differing viewpoint. Here, in the United States, we see this played out daily in our political discourse; we're convinced we're right and the other person is wrong. Sometimes, we even go as far as to demonize the other person.

Dr. Stephen Covey, in his book *7 Habits of Highly Effective People*, says it this way:

> If you're like most people, you probably seek first to be understood; you want to get your point across. And in doing so, you may ignore the other person completely, pretend that you're listening, selectively hear only certain parts of the conversation or attentively focus on only the words being said, but miss the meaning entirely. So why does this happen? Because most people listen with the intent to reply, not to understand. You listen to yourself as you prepare in your mind what you are going to say, the questions you are going to ask, etc. You filter everything you hear through your life experiences, your frame of reference. You check what you hear against your autobiography and see how it measures up. And consequently, you

decide prematurely what the other person means before he/she finishes communicating.

We're assuming here that your audience is at a different place than where you want them to be. But before attempting to move them to where you want them to go, try to understand why they are where they are. Keep in mind there's another side to the story. And when you're willing to listen and understand, you're on the road to making a solid connection.

Now, I want to present five techniques for connecting: humor, compassion, empathy, storytelling, and authenticity. Let's go through each one, as well as a few tips for employing them.

1. HUMOR

Many professional speakers have had some variation on this exchange: "Do I have to use humor in my keynote address?" "Only if you want to get paid." People respond to humor. So many people are living stressful lives that offering them the opportunity to escape, laugh, and see life differently is a true gift.

Perhaps my favorite resource for applying humor in persuasion is Judy Carter's *The Comedy Bible*. In this book, Carter gives step-by-step guidance on adding humor to any form of communication. She suggests that comedy is all around us. We just get so busy with life that we fail to notice. So keep your eyes open. Look for, as Carter puts it, "weirdness, stupidity, and oddness" wherever you happen to be. Keep a journal and record what you observe.

2. COMPASSION

Compassion is awareness of where another person is, and includes a desire to help change that situation—assuming, of course, it's not an ideal situation. And compassion will challenge us to leave our perspective and seek to understand what's happening in the other person's life.

Why is this important? It allows you, the persuader, to go to where your audience is, understand their perspective, and then lead them to the decision you want them to make.

3. EMPATHY

While compassion moves us to understand and alleviate negative aspects of another's life, empathy takes it one step further. Empathy allows us to feel vicariously what others are going through.

Perhaps this is one of the greatest elements missing in today's political discourse. We lack empathy for others.

I grew up in rural North Carolina, but after graduate school, I made the move to a larger city. My adopted hometown has come out of the recession much better than where I was raised. Jobs abound, the housing market is strong, and the quality of life is impressive. It's easy to live in a bubble, thinking every-one is experiencing life in a similar manner. But it's not true.

In the heat of the 2016 elections, I spent an afternoon grilling and drinking with people living in rural areas of my state. I was reminded of how strong, resilient this community is. But I also began to see a people who haven't seen prosperity the way the state's urban core has. They've endured and survived. But they feel they're being left behind and are voiceless.

Maybe it's because I come from a rural community, but at the end of that afternoon, my connection was more than a desire to help change their situations; I felt their pain. Their suffering, concerns, anxiety became mine.

And that was my connection. Listening to their stories opened my eyes to empathy. And though we were in different places in life and viewpoints, we connected.

4. STORYTELLING

One of my favorite and most productive ways to persuade is by telling stories. I would venture to say that storytelling is the quickest way for me to connect with my audience. I can make an emotional connection rather quickly as I share my perspective through a story. And I'm more likely to persuade if I've connected.

Often when we're constructing our argument for persuasion, we structure in cause and effect. That's how people naturally think. In its simplest form, a story is that connection between cause and effect. In other words, this happened, and here is the result.

Why does this work so well for me? I think it's because stories well-told don't actually tell—they show. So, often when we are trying to persuade others, we fall into the trap of just telling people what we want them to do. Often, there's a natural push-back from our audience. Storytelling removes the "telling" part and "shows" your audience. And people generally prefer you show and not just tell them.

I think the most compelling and connecting stories are those we share of our own mistakes and failures. If you can be honest about your own shortcomings, you'll become more relatable to your audience. Let's face it: We've all screwed up. As you share your own story, your audience will connect with your perceived failure, helping you persuade them to your perspective. Dale Carnegie says, "Speakers who talk about what life has taught them never fail to keep the attention of their listeners."

Just this past week, I opened a keynote speech with a personal story. I felt alive, passionate, and excited to speak; but more importantly, I was aware that people were fully engaged. I had their attention; they anxiously awaited the unfolding of my story. They smiled. They laughed. And although I knew almost no one in the room, I connected in a meaningful way.

Like humor, I think storytelling transcends the present. Your audience can experience journeys and emotions, all while remaining firmly in their seats. Told well, a story can capti-vate and help transform thinking. It's a very non-threatening way to share a viewpoint.

A few tips on telling stories:

- ◦ Your story should have at least one moment of truth. This is sometimes referred to as the "aha" moment.

- ◦ Sometimes in advocacy campaigns, proponents will share stories to help the audience gain an emotional connection to the cause. If this is your intent, one piece of advice: Make sure you tell the story of a single person, not a group. And it's even more effective when you can share at least the first name of the person.

- ◦ Make sure your story has a clear meaning. We've probably all heard stories, only to reach the end, questioning what the purpose of the story was.

- ◦ Keep the storyline moving at a rapid pace. One way to do this is to remove any and all unnecessary aspects. If it isn't necessary to the message, toss it. If bombarded with unnecessary information, not only will your audience grow bored and/or distracted, they may well have a difficult time understanding your intent.

- ◦ Use simple, heartfelt words, not overly complicated ones.

5. AUTHENTICITY

When working with the millennial generation, I'll argue that authenticity isn't an option, it's required. In general, millennials demand what is real and true and reject the fake. And regardless of the age of your audience, there are few things that will move them more quickly than opening your heart to show you care.

A quick caution: If *you're* trying to be authentic, stop. People can see through the attempts. Authenticity is about being, not trying.

I fully understand people being afraid to be open and real. For years, that was my life. I felt like if I allowed people to see who I really was, I would be rejected. But what I discovered was the opposite: opening up and being transparent deeply connected me.

Here are a few things to consider in striving for authenticity:

Ask questions

I've heard people ask questions to show they care. But I think I'd flip that around. I think if you care, you'll naturally ask questions without being prompted to do so. And if you search deep inside and don't care, that's an entirely different discussion.

Accept that you make mistakes

You're human, and you're not perfect. I can't even begin to count how much time I spent in therapy to accept this fact. I was raised in a home that expected perfection, and perfection all the time. Toss in a heavy dose of being constantly reminded that what people think of me is paramount, and you can see the recipe for disaster. Try accepting that you're human. You will make mistakes, and most likely people around you won't judge you for simple mistakes.

Be present

Everyone seems to be saying, "Be present" these days. But I'm going to say it anyway. Be present. People know if you're not in the moment with them. They won't connect if they don't feel you're right there with them.

And at the risk of being that "get-off-of-my-lawn" crank, let me add that constantly being on your device when you're with others definitely doesn't reinforce that you're present. Try putting it down and giving that person your full attention.

Another industry expert's perspective:

> Whether speaking to an audience of one or one thousand, we must set ego aside and recognize what is important to the other person. This conversation took place over twenty years ago but remains a constant reminder of that point.
>
> I'll never forget visiting with my hospice patient, Ned Johnson. We had a wonderful connection, and I knew that he valued my visits as a chaplain.
>
> One day, I said, "Ned, you've got a special glow about you today."
>
> He grinned. "Yeah, I do."
>
> I asked what was going on.
>
> "Oh, man," he said, "I had the best visit yesterday."
>
> Well, that took me down a peg. I hadn't been to see Ned the day before, so I knew his great visit wasn't with me! I thought, "Okay, maybe the nurse or the social worker had come."
>
> Mustering up cheerfulness, I asked, "Who was here, Ned?"

"My volunteer."

Wow! Ned just knocked out the whole clinical staff. Now the volunteer is his favorite!

Okay. It was time to swallow my pride and learn what deep topic had been covered since Ned and I still had a few more big conversations to go. "Well, Ned, what did you talk about?"

"Talk? We didn't talk about anything. We watched a football game!"

Carlos, Ned's quiet, big-hearted volunteer, showed his caring through actions rather than words. For one afternoon, he gave Ned the chance to do what he craved: to be normal and watch football with another guy.

That was the best connection.

Becky Sansbury
BeckySansbury.com

Ready for the next step? Let's talk about how to position your message.

Questions for Reflection

1. How does making a connection help you persuade?

2. How do you know if you've made a connection?

3. Of the techniques listed, do you naturally gravitate toward one device more than others? If so, how and why?

4. What's the correlation between helping others find their win and making a connection?

5. Have you ever sensed someone was manipulating a connection with you? How did you know? How did that feel?

Chapter 8

POSITIONING YOUR MESSAGE

"Leadership is the art of getting someone else to do something you want done because he wants to do it."

—Dwight D. Eisenhower—

Before we look at some strategies to help you position your message for a favorable response, I encourage you to first look inside yourself.

How do you approach asking? Are you an asker or a guesser? Let's talk about both.

Some people are fine with asking questions without regard for the outcome. In other words, they're fine with asking anything at all and are readily willing to accept no.

Other people fall into the guesser category. Those in this category avoid making "the ask" without being pretty certain the answer will be yes. People in this category will often put out feelers to better predict the outcome. These people often ease into the ask, or don't even have to make it at all. By edging closer and closer to the desired outcome, their audience will often be persuaded through this strategic, indirect approach to persuading.

Have you ever asked someone to marry you? If so, what was your approach? This answer is a huge indicator of your style. For me, when I proposed, I was a guesser. I put out multiple feelers. I tested the water. And, in fact, we ended up planning a wedding without the traditional proposal. And that path worked for us.

Understanding your style will help you best prepare for your "ask." Like my wedding proposal (or lack thereof), you may end up getting your "yes" without ever asking! Or if you are an "asker," I suggest you make overly certain you've taken all necessary steps before you officially make the "ask."

Now that you better understand how you ask questions, it's time to think through your strategy of positioning your message. Let's explore three ways of positioning:

1. LOSS AVERSION VS. PROSPECT THEORY

Loss aversion is the theory that contends people prefer to avoid losses more than they do making gains.

When positioning your ask, you should consider an approach that suggests what your user will lose instead of what they will gain.

For example, if you put a time limit on a special discount, messaging about losing this discount will most likely catch your users attention and prompt them to act. Or if you message that they will lose access to something, you can also likely prompt users to decide in your favor.

2. EMOTION VS. LOGIC (FEAR, HATE, ANGER)

**"People don't buy for logical reasons.
They buy for emotional reasons."
—Zig Ziglar—**

Those of us who process information in a more logical manner often likewise frame our asks logically. And while, for some, that will work, in general, people will tend to gravitate to their emotions in decision-making.

Though it admittedly sounds bad, people will often take action based on fear quicker than any other emotion.

We *feel* before we think.

What happens when you intersect loss aversion with fear? You get a powerful tool to persuade. Consider the 2016 U.S. presidential election.

One of the most powerful ads of that political cycle was one produced by the National Rifle Association. This ad was intended to make people fearful of Hillary Clinton, alleging she would take away their guns.

The ad was a $5M buy, the NRA's largest of that cycle. That tells you they were banking on the success of combining loss aversion with fear.

In the 30-second ad, a woman is awakened from her sleep by the sound of glass breaking, and immediately calls 911.

The voiceover states: "She'll call 911. Average response time: 11 minutes. Too late."

Realizing she's in danger, with no help coming, she reaches for the safe, enters the code, and reaches to remove a handgun. But, all of a sudden, the safe and the gun vanish.

The voiceover continues: "She keeps a firearm in this safe for protection. But Hillary Clinton could take away her right to self-defense. And with Supreme Court justices, Hillary can."

With a cut then to the home wrapped in crime scene tape and blue lights piercing the night, the narrator concludes: "Don't let Hillary leave you protected with nothing but a phone."

Why was this commercial so effective and worthy of the largest ad buy for the National Rifle Association for that cycle? Fear. And it worked.

3. BINARY VS. NON-BINARY OPTIONS

Sometimes, we think our ask has to be black and white, yes or no. So, in response, we structure our ask as an all-or-nothing deal. But does it have to be? Or are there multiple potential options that might work? This is your opportunity to be creative; find a way that everyone wins. Expand your own thinking, as to the possibilities.

And while I will agree that often times the decision is a yes or no, I don't think it always has to be the case, nor should it. If you understand what you want and what your user wants, can't you find a way that both of you can walk away happy?

On a public affairs campaign I ran, the bill had to be approached in a creative manner. Had we positioned this bill to be a yes or no, it would likely have failed. There were areas of the state that would never be in favor, and so their legislators would have voted against it. And there were areas of the state that were begging for the bill's success. So, the bill's sponsors decided to make the adoption within municipalities opt in instead of automatic. That way, legislators representing districts that would not be in favor could vote yes without impacting their own districts. The result? The bill became law. And with very little pushback.

If you're making a binary ask, it's important not to back your audience into a corner too soon because it's really hard to move them out once you've boxed them in. Give them lots of flexibility to move and change their viewpoint.

You see, sometimes, we push people to make a decision way too soon. I suggest you give time to receive and process information. Early on, it's fine to test the waters or see what they are thinking. In fact, it can be very helpful to provide additional, clarifying information as needed. Sharing information in this manner can greatly increase your chances of persuading. However, if you push for an answer too soon, you might get an answer you don't want. And it's a lot harder to move someone once a decision has been made. So make it easier on yourself and postpone the ask.

Ready for the next step? Let's talk about how to craft your call to action.

Questions for Reflection

1. What does positioning your message mean to you?

2. Are you more of an asker or a guesser?

3. Why do you think emotion outperforms logic?

4. Are there ways to use emotion and logic? If so, what are they?

5. Which best motivates you, loss aversion or prospect theory? Why?

Chapter 9

CRAFTING YOUR CALL TO ACTION

"I've learned that people will forget what you said, people will forget what you did, but people will never forget how you made them feel."

—Maya Angelou—

With your message crafted and positioned, it's time to make the ask. Up to this point, you've crafted your message, you've thought through how you can help them win, you've sought out a connection, and you've positioned your ask in the best manner. So, it's time for the next step. It's time to create your call to action.

So what exactly is a call to action?

According to Dictionary.com, a call to action is "an exhortation or stimulus to do something in order to achieve an aim or deal with a problem." As in, "He ended his speech with a call to action."

In a marketing context, according to Merriam-Webster, this means "a piece of content intended to induce a viewer, reader, or listener to perform a specific act, typically taking the form of an instruction or directive (e.g. buy now or click here)."

Fundamental to the call to action is recognizing that you're asking someone to do something. The primary questions to think through are: "When do you want them to do it?" "Why should they do it?" and "Why is it to their benefit to do it?"

If you've successfully reached this point of the ask, you should already fully understand the "why." In making that ask, be certain that your why focuses on what problem you intend to solve. People are most likely to say yes when you're offering to solve a real problem they face. And they'll often pay a premium price for you to do it.

But you must make certain they understand the value you're bringing to them.

It's also important to maintain a consistent voice throughout the entire process.

And another thing—before the actual ask, there's a very important question to answer: "Have you adequately addressed any concerns they may have?" That could look like any unresolved questions have been answered. You want to make sure the audience has all questions answered and all concerns addressed. At this stage, there should be some type of relationship established. This relationship will help you ensure your audience is in the best place possible to make a decision.

Here are 13 tips to help you craft a call to action that your audience can't resist:

1. MAKE YOUR ASK CLEAR.

We've probably all been there: You meet with someone, you know they want something from you, but you leave unclear of the ask.

Your ask should tell them what to do, when to do it, and why they should do it.

2. BE SURE TO USE A STRONG ACTION VERB.

3. MAKE IT PERSONAL; USE "YOU" AND "YOUR."

We talked, in Chapter 6, about helping others find their win so that you win, also. In your call to action, you, once again, get to put this powerful tool to work. Using the pronouns "you" and "your" help your audience focus on why this matters to them. Remember, they're asking—whether explicitly or implicitly—"What's in it for me?"

And try to stay away from nouns and/or pronouns that talk about you and what you want ("me" and "my").

4. COMMUNICATE VALUE

What is the value your proposition brings to your audience? Again, how does it fit into one of the health, wealth, or relationship buckets? And keep in mind the value will be different for different audiences. What is your audience's need? Use this to craft a clear value proposition.

5. BE CLEVER

People often become tense about making decisions. Finding a clever approach can help break this stiffness. It also makes your pitch unique, distinctive.

6. EXPRESS EMOTION

We talked about emotion earlier in our messaging. It's time to dust that back off.

7. CREATE A SENSE OF URGENCY

Use a countdown clock on a landing page. Announce the point at which you'll "take away" the offer. Using time-sensitive words is another way to do this.

8. USE A SINGULAR CALL TO ACTION

Oftentimes, there may be several actions you want a person to take. But it's best to present them one at a time ("Sign our petition," "Share on social," "Like us on FB," etc.).

9. USE STRONG, PRECISE, PUNCHY LANGUAGE

Too often, CTA's are mushy. This type of language actually hinders your ability to persuade. Betsy Talbot, on her site BetsyTalbot.com, offers some great examples of revising mushy language into strong language:

Before	**After**
You are invited	Reserve your seat now
Click here	Tell me more
Submit	See my results
Register	Start my free trial
Leave a comment	Tell us how it worked for you
Visit our FAQ	Find answers here
Contact us	Tell us about your problem
Schedule a call	Book your free mini-consult

10. REDUCE RISK

It's not unlikely that your audience is weighing out the benefits of taking the action against the risks involved. Think through those potential perceived risks. Then find ways to reduce or eliminate them.

Could you offer two weeks for free? Money back within the first thirty days?

Your goal is to eliminate anxiety, allowing the audience to make the decision worry free.

11. ESTABLISH SCARCITY

We all want what we can't have. Your audience is much more likely to want what you're offering if they're concerned there may not be enough for them. In fact, it'll make them want it more if they fear (emotion) they won't be able to get it.

12. POWER OF A CROWD

Social proof can be one of the greatest tools in developing an effective CTA. If others are doing something, we tend to want to do it. So think through the power of the crowd to see how others could help persuade your audience.

13. MAKE IT EASY

People are busy, and all around them are distractions. Once they're ready to follow through on your CTA, make it as easy as possible to close the deal. This is extremely important with digital purchases. Keep all unnecessary roadblocks out of the way.

With these tools in your toolbox, you'll have exactly what you need to craft a call to action your user can't resist. Just be sure to figure out which one(s) will work best for your audience.

Ready for the next step? Let's talk about how to become an industry expert.

Questions for Reflection

1. "Asks" are often fuzzy, unclear. What defines a "clear" ask?

2. Think back to the simple message you created in the reflection section of Chapter 3. What is it you want your audience to do?

3. Can you think of instances in which you may have multiple calls to action? If so, how would you move users through them to get the ultimate action you want?

4. When looking through your call to action, have you clearly defined its value to your audience?

5. Have you focused on sales features or the problem you solve?

Chapter 10

BECOMING AN INDUSTRY EXPERT

"Persuasion is achieved by the speaker's personal character when the speech is so spoken as to make us think him credible. We believe good men more fully and more readily than others: this is true generally whatever the question is, and absolutely true where exact certainty is impossible and opinions are divided."

—Aristotle—

One of the most significant elements of persuasion gets overlooked—and it really shouldn't.

That element is this: Becoming an industry expert is your secret weapon in rising above your competition.

First, a word of caution: Never consider yourself sufficiently expert that you stop gaining expertise. View life as a continuous learning experience.

Earlier, I discussed the steps that anyone should go through in the buying process. To recap: When closing a deal, I operate in three steps: know, like, trust. These steps must be well-defined and carried out in order.

One of the most potentially valuable tools in gaining that ultimate trust is establishing industry expertise. As the expert, most likely, people will instinctively trust you.

You've probably heard the saying: "It's all about who you

know." Well, I disagree. I think it's more about who knows you and what they think of you.

People often consider a corporate or personal brand to be a logo. It's not. Actually, a brand is held by others. A brand is how others perceive you or your company. And your role is to give them clues, as to how you want to be known.

A logo is one of those clues. But so is your messaging, your photos, your color palette, your facial expressions and body language, your publications, and more. There's a wide range of clues that potential clients use to frame up your brand.

And perhaps the most potent means of conveying clues to the people you're trying to persuade is to be viewed as that industry expert.

This isn't about gaining a mass audience; it's about establishing yourself within your targeted audience. And there are so many resources at your disposal to gain and maintain that trust.

I'm presently working with a wellness group that has asked me to design a curriculum for wellness experts who are embedded in a company. The objective is to help raise their profile within that company. It's a niche area, and the trick is to arrive as the expert—someone to be trusted. They'll then seek you out, rather than vice versa: "He's the guru; he knows. I want to know more."

Establishing yourself as an industry expert means you've mastered your niche area of expertise, found your targeted audience, and you understand how to reach it with compelling messages—in your own, unique voice.

Ever listen to Gary Vaynerchuk or Grant Cardone? They have very distinctive voices. A distinctive tone sets you apart from everyone else in this crowded field; it builds trust and helps determine how you'll persuade.

Finding your voice will come over time. But you need to start where you are and allow your voice to reveal itself through your work. Then, once you've embraced your true voice, I encourage you to keep it consistent. Be you. You'll discover your own unique ways of communicating ideas to your audience.

So how do you get there? How do you become the industry expert? Here are three critical steps.

1. UNDERSTAND YOUR SKILLS.

What expertise do you have? What are you good at doing? What do you love to do? What are your top three strengths?

I'm convinced we all have areas in which we know more than others. Let's frame it up this way: What issues do your skills solve? The answer should fall into one of three buckets: health, wealth, relationships.

There's a lot of competition out there, a lot of noise, and making your voice ring through the noise din is no easy task. You have to differentiate yourself, or as Nilofer Merchant puts it, find your "onlyness." Your voice doesn't need to resonate with everyone—you don't need everyone as a client—but you need to find your niche.

2. FIGURE OUT YOU.

Some people refer to this as your unique selling point, or USP. Merchant defines onlyness thusly:

> Onlyness is that thing that only that one individual can bring to a situation. It includes the journey and passions of each human. Onlyness is fundamentally about honoring each person: first as we view ourselves and second as we are valued. Each of us is standing in a spot that no one else occupies. That unique point of view is born of our accumulated experience, perspective, and vision. Some of those experiences are not as "perfect" as we might want, but even those experiences are a source for what you create.

Think through your onlyness. If you can't define it, you'll never stand out. (Judy Carter's book *The Message of You* is another highly recommended resource.)

3. FIND YOUR AUDIENCE.

Don't let this overwhelm you. Again, it's not about winning over everyone. It's not about mass. It's about niche. You simply need to take ownership of a piece of the pie. Look for fallow ground in the market; look for what's missing. This is where you should consider planting yourself.

My public affairs and communications firm is presently working with an insurance lobbyist, Ben. Ben is already an industry expert. But he's always worked in public service; he hasn't yet debuted his expertise in the marketplace.

Ben is respected for his experience working in administrative government, having established himself among his colleagues as an expert on the healthcare and insurance industries.

Ben recognized there is no single source for information on the legislative process addressing these industries—industries that affect us all. He's identified a gap, a need—one that he's well qualified to fill.

He understands who his audience is: legislators, healthcare and insurance specialists, other lobbyists, the business community. He has the credibility. But he must first build his brand.

Ben is in a good position: When you've gained the expertise, identified your target market, and there's clearly a gap in knowledge—that's the trifecta. Now, it's a matter of getting his message out there: "I've been there. I have the expertise. I can guide you."

The launching point for Ben—as for all industry experts—was defining his space. In their book *Blue Ocean Strategy*, W. Chan Kim and Renée Mauborgne define "blue water" as the place where you can find success; "red water," conversely, is the shark-infested zone.

You need to find the place where others are not—your niche market, devoid of sharks. When you find this place, this market, you're set for success. You're confident in your skills, you've identified your uniqueness, you've determined your niche audience. Now, you must capture this audience.

How? For the most part, you'll do this work online. Most everyone can engage with their market online. There are so many resources at your avail.

For Ben, we are, of course, employing Twitter, LinkedIn, Instagram, Facebook. We're also leveraging Ben's considerable email database. He's now putting out a newsletter recapping what's happening in the legislature. He's establishing himself as the go-to guy, and he's building a client base.

I can't overemphasize the importance of embracing the full potential of your online tools. I meet people from all over the globe every single day through LinkedIn. With LinkedIn, I can hone in tightly on the people with whom I want to connect. I can identify my audience.

I find that people are very open to making those connections through LinkedIn. Typically, they're using it because they want to broaden their connections. So—assuming you're adding value and convincing them you're worth their time—it's an easy way to connect.

I'm not trying to attract everyone; I'm focusing on those I want to pull in. Just having them as part of my network—and as I regularly post updates—allows me to strengthen my brand and reinforce my message. It's not like I'm constantly emailing them. It's like a feather touch.

Each of these online tools has its own particular assets. Twitter, for example, is a great place to get the media's attention.

If you're working in public affairs, or anywhere in the political sphere, you'll learn that reporters live on Twitter. It's a great way to reach them.

We've discussed, in these pages, how to craft a message. Where you take it is equally critical. You have to determine what platform(s) you'll use to get that message out to your audience. In determining what communications platforms to use, ask this question: "Where is my target market?" Then get yourself out there.

And be mindful that your audience is not only the people you seek out on these platforms but also those who have liked or commented on your posts. As you begin to build content, your audience will grow—exponentially.

Keeping your brand out there is so important. As much as McDonald's is engrained in our culture, we're still bombarded each day with ads for those golden arches. As ubiquitous as the Apple logo is in our homes, office, and coffeeshops, there it is, too, unceasingly in the media.

Online tools are noninvasive means of keeping your brand in front of your targeted audience. It takes some work. But the tools are out there, and they're affordable.

But before you push out your first piece of content, I want you to commit to consistently showing up. You have to be in the conversation, all the time. This is why I love and continue to use scheduled and automated posts. Don't go ghost on your audience. Show up regularly.

With that commitment, you're ready to start sharing content. Here are some suggestions.

Post an article. This article can be posted on your blog. If you don't have a blog, no worries. There are sites like medium. com where you can set up an account in less than two minutes and begin publishing. You can also write a post on LinkedIn or your other existing social sites.

Post a video. Now, I realize that creating a video seems intimidating to a lot of people. You want a level of professionalism that well represents your brand. Producing videos can be expensive, but it doesn't have to be. In fact, your videos will probably gain more traction if they're less polished and more authentic—professional and authentic. I encourage you to strongly consider this option.

Record a podcast. You may well find that your target market regularly consumes podcasts. I'm one of those people. Almost anytime I'm in my car, I have a podcast playing. If you decide to move forward with podcasting, check out Clammr for converting lengthy podcasts into short sound bites for sharing on social media.

Broadcast a live event. Facebook Live is currently gaining a lot of traction. It's a quick, easy way to test messaging—to explore new ideas, see how people respond, and make decisions about building out the content. Why not give it a try?

Share on social media. Hands down, social media is the largest driver of traffic to my website. And Twitter champions all my social networks. I realize social media can be time consuming, and often people question the return on investment.

Since I know it brings value, but I have limited time, I use MeetEdgar to manage my social media. In just a few hours a month, I can upload all my social posts, and I determine the distribution time. If you're heavy into Pinterest, try scheduling with Tailwind. Or Grum, Kistagram, or Onlypult for Instagram. And Facebook has a built-in scheduler.

Keep in mind that you should always include an image with your posts. I often use branded personal images. You may want to select a stunning, relevant image from a service such as Over, Quick, Typorama, or Enlight. You can add captions instantly from your mobile. And if your target audience is into Instagram, create a beautiful image with a striking headline. Also, consider using sponsored posts in Facebook if you determine it's worth the investment.

Brand your short links when sharing on social media. My links are all shortened with my name. My current favorite is Short.cm. Links look like this: http://jefftippett.co/inKUqx. You can also track conversion rates using this service.

So what does all this have to do with persuasion? One of the most effective tools for successfully persuading is to be that industry expert. And how are you establishing yourself as that expert? You take your skill sets, you build your audience, you find that niche, and you keep your brand in front of them.

Another industry expert's perspective:

> What comes to your mind when you hear about Steve Jobs, Brian Tracy, Sheryl Sandberg, or Stephen King?
>
> They are all great examples of people recognized as industry experts. They positioned their message and brand so effectively and skillfully that it gives them an advantage over others. People like these can establish their connection as a trusted authority with their audience, employees, or followers, in an instant. *Effective positioning* is the secret sauce to stand out, expand your reach, maintain an edge, and thrive in a crowded industry. Positioning is the creation of a focused brand message and sharing it with your tribe on a consistent basis.
>
> The first step is to have clarity around your purpose, your vision, your mission, and your values. With clarity comes congruence. Then you must deeply understand the hearts and minds of the industry and the people you serve. When your promise is in alignment with your values and customers' needs, you can craft a personalized and meaningful message, to which your audience is compelled to engage. Further, this compelling message helps build your brand story that creates a community of people that are deeply connected and proud to belong to.
>
> The second step is to build marketing systems that work for your brand and yield consistent and predictable results. For example, if you decide to rely heavily on content marketing, then it is essential to have specific ways to communicate consistently with your audience. Different techniques of building your brand communication with your audience could include writing a book, speaking, weekly newsletters, online video series, Facebook lives, podcasts, or webinars. The list may seem overwhelming, but the key is to know what your audience is consuming, choose those few mediums, and focus

only on them. By building your unique and unprecedented platform strategy to solidify your brand's relationship with your market, you are positioning yourself as an authority.

One of the most valuable strategies to establish you as an industry expert is to write a book. Authoring a book on your expertise gives you instant legitimacy in your profession. It also gives you a tremendous sense of accomplishment, but that is not the end game. Your book becomes a dynamic component of your brand. It can open doors that otherwise are not available. You can share it with colleagues, clients, and potential customers, to give them greater insight into who you are and what you do. It is an excellent starting point with which to speak at conferences or other public forums, to further get your message out. You can double your success with social media and the different ways you promote yourself with a book. Indeed, a book is the impetus for some professionals to begin actively branding them-selves. Start observing other influencers that have written books, including industry experts who do "Ted Talks," speak at conferences, or you find on YouTube.

Let's review how books helped shape my influence. Initially, as I transitioned from my corporate career to establishing my business in leadership coaching, I was offered an oppor-tunity to contribute to an anthology. From that one chapter, I went on to write a series of leadership and entrepreneurial books addressing the market's needs. Several of my books achieved bestselling status. My books allowed my audience to experience my coaching, shortening the time between the "getting to know me" and the "trusting cycle." Not only did the books impact people but they also became the source to grow my coaching business. The books helped me expand my reach in several ways, like getting on podcasts, local tv shows, magazines, and becoming a contributor to several publications including Forbes. It's time to put yourself on the literary Mt. Rushmore. If my clients and I could do it, so can you!

The last step is to develop a purposeful relationship with industry influencers. Start with giving, without expecting anything in return. When you lead with giving, you form a connection with the influencers. Once they see you as a giver, and not a taker, most influencers will support what you ask, especially if you ask with humility.

A cohesive, consistent message and brand, with a focused and targeted platform, will establish you as the authority that invites your audience in with welcoming gloves.

Divya Parekh
DivyaParekh.com

Ready for the next step? Let's talk about a few other things you need to consider.

Questions for Reflection

1. What are your top three skills?

2. What is unique about you? (This could be education, personal story, background, spots no one else occupies.)

3. Who is your target audience? I encourage you to think very targeted. Drill down deep.

4. How do you find your target market?

5. How do you message your audience? And remain top of mind?

Chapter 11

A FEW ADDITIONAL THINGS

"Many of life's failures are people who did not realize how close they were to success when they gave up."

—Thomas A. Edison—

Before we wrap up, there are a few final considerations I think could be helpful to you as you become a master at persuasion.

1. THERE'S MORE THAN ONE PATH

While it would certainly simplify things if one path for persuading others was perfect for everyone, it doesn't work that way. If that were true, there would be a single book that has all the answers we could buy and be done with this.

There's not some magical approach to a quick success. We're dealing with human beings, not robots. And though, generally speaking, a particular approach may work, you have to find your own way of approaching.

Think through your options. What's the best way to craft the message? What's the best way to position your message?

What's the best call to action? And when determining the best path, I encourage you (once again) to focus on your audience. At this point, you should know your audience intimately. Making your decisions audience-centered will give you the best opportunity for success.

But even with the best and most informed decisions, don't be surprised if not every step produces your desired results. Be willing to make course corrections, as necessary.

2. PERSUASION DOESN'T FOLLOW A LINEAR PATH

The sales funnel is dead. People choose their own paths. They bounce around. They take steps with you, then back off. They go ghost. They then magically reappear, perhaps after seeing something new you've posted on social media or in an email.

3. THESE ARE GENERALLY ACCEPTED PRACTICES

My goal in these preceding chapters has been to show you what works—generally speaking. But, again, it's not a one-size-fits-all proposition. If you can understand the theories presented here, you can then think through the potential variables and test to see what works best for you. Make it your own.

5. KNOW YOUR AUDIENCE

I've talked a lot in this book about connecting with your audience and about being focused on helping your audience win. It's crucial for you to know your audience. You have to understand what they need, how they make decisions, what motivates them. Your approach will vary based on your audience. It's essential that you come to know them.

6. TEST

Test everything—your messaging, your delivery platforms, your positioning, your call to action. Yes, everything.

Before rolling out your messaging, test it. Try delivering it as if you're explaining it to a child. As condescending as this may sound, I encourage you to examine whether your messaging is simple enough for a child to understand. The first step toward persuasion is to simplify your message. Make it easy on your audience.

Share your messaging with people you know well. Float it past them and gather responses before taking it to others. I think it's especially helpful to share it with people who have no knowledge of the subject matter.

Finally, consider this: You now possess the superpower of persuasion. That's right: You have a powerful toolbox that will increase your effectiveness, empower you to reach your goals, and help you positively impact your organization.

Just keep your focus on your audience. Solve problems for them. Show them you care. Bring success—and your audience will champion you as a superhero.

Ready for the next step? Let's talk about why trust matters.

Chapter 12

TRUST IS CRUCIAL

"Trust has to be earned, and should come only after the passage of time."
—Arthur Ashe—

This is, perhaps, the most important chapter in this book. If you master every skill in every chapter, but others don't trust you, you won't persuade. Period.

Most people think of trust in terms of the things we do to earn it. And while, yes, I'll focus there, as well, we need to start much deeper. The foundation for building trust is your motivations, what's in your heart, the spirit in which you eventually do those things to earn it. A well-trained salesperson can easily fool others for a while, but in the end, I don't think it's sustainable.

I encourage you to pause and look within. I believe that others' trust in you begins with who you are as a person and what your intentions are. And, ultimately, no amount of smooth talking can make up for the wrong intentions.

At the outset, most of your audience will either be neutral or slightly disinclined to trust you. But you now have what you need to begin earning their trust. If you took my "Industry

Expert" chapter seriously, answered the questions, and have started building out your personal brand, you have a leg up in this process. You're working from a solid foundation for building trust.

In Chapter 6, "Helping Others Find Their Win (So You Win)," we briefly discussed intentions. Now, in this chapter, it's important to hit this concept head-on. We have to check our motivations and determine what drives us. Is our primary focus on ourselves and what we want in life or do we place a priority and importance on others. Just this simple, yet often overlooked mindset, can make drastic changes in how people perceive us and ultimately our ability to persuade them.

Self-examination is good, and a conversation with those who know you could be even more beneficial. (But don't start with your best friends. Because they love you, they may lack objectivity.)

Below are 10 tips to explore and then use for your discussion with others. And at the end of this chapter, I've put them in a concise list to ease the logistics of that discussion.

1. BE CONSISTENT

It takes multiple interactions for your audience to begin to get a feel for who you are. These could be F2F meetings, phone calls, or social media communication. And you'll need precise consistency for people to begin to fully understand you, know your story, and begin to trust you. Often, even the slightest deviation can set you back.

Since I've brought up social media, let's pause there a moment. Every interaction—whether posting, sharing, or commenting—gives your audience clues to your brand presence. And unless your social accounts are locked down tight (and even then, your audience can often still find you), every action matters. I would argue that every single post—no exceptions—has to support the brand you are creating. Any deviation can derail your quest to earn the trust of others.

2. DELIVER AS PROMISED

We've probably all had someone promise us a deliverable—whether a creative asset, meeting time, contract, phone call, email, etc.—and not, in fact, deliver. Failing to deliver as promised can harm your brand and the fragile trust you're building with your audience.

We're often so eager to please that we commit to things that, realistically, we know we can't deliver. In the moment, that promise feels comforting. It's nice to think you're going to fulfill someone's wants or needs. But while your audience may be happy in the moment that you said yes to their request—and that makes you feel good, as well—nobody's going to feel good when expectations aren't met. Overpromising will not only likely disappoint, it will set back your quest for trust.

It's better then to under-promise and over-deliver. If your audience is asking for something, and you know you can't deliver, manage expectations. Explain the rationale for why you can't deliver. Even better, frame your response in a way that shows why your decision is best for them.

I recently had a speakers' bureau reach out to me because they wanted to represent me. I responded that I was interested, and asked the next steps. Well, the decision and onboarding process was extremely laborious. And I knew that current demands on my time would not allow me to complete that process in the given timeframe.

Given that I do have interest in working with this bureau, I explained to them my current commitments. I told them I wanted to complete all the forms and provide what they needed in a thorough manner. Further, I told them I wanted to give them quality assets, and I couldn't do that at the present moment.

I then told them when I could reasonably expect to get everything to them, and they accepted my timeline.

Now contrast that approach to overpromising. Had I done that, and not provided the requested information on time, we would have begun what could be a mutually financially beneficial arrangement on the wrong foot. And if this bureau can't trust me with the initial process, certainly they won't be able to trust me when it matters to their clients.

Under-promise. Over-deliver. Every time. It's a winning formula.

3. BE OPEN AND AUTHENTIC

I acknowledge that being open and authentic within the business community often raises eyebrows. Most of us have been trained to leave our personal self outside the door when we walk into the office. I disagree with that.

But let me add this disclaimer (one you've heard from me before): Know your audience. Know to what extent they're willing to "get real with you"—where the boundaries lie.

To the extent that your audience is willing to be open and authentic, I encourage you to respond to the full extent to which you're comfortable. This authenticity will allow your audience to trust you more profoundly. Besides, you don't want them wondering what you might be hiding.

Of all the tips for developing earning the trust of others, perhaps authenticity has been the most challenging for me. I perfected relationships with a shield in hand keeping others at a safe distance; I was the master of keeping people from getting too close. And I was blind to the harm it was doing to my relationships.

When I was in middle school I formed a friendship with a new neighbor. We had both recently moved into a new neighborhood. We both were active in music and church life. And we had a lot of fun hanging out. In fact, he was probably my closest friend.

Like other kids our age, we rode bikes, watched TV, and had sleepovers. After all, childhoods are meant to be fun, carefree.

While the other aspects of hanging out and playing as young boys were totally normal, the second time I slept over negatively impacted my life. Forever.

Without recalling and discussing too many negative details, my friend's father, a Southern Baptist pastor, sexually abused me. It happened several times, and I was blinded to its effects on my life.

For decades, I replayed this scenario in my head; I had only been able to speak it to a few people in my life. And sharing with those people was extremely painful.

And over time, after surfacing over and over, the pain of this childhood experience finally pushed me to get professional help. I needed to understand and find clarity. And in this clarity, I began to understand that, as a result of this unnecessary childhood event, I built a cage of protection around myself. I had tons of friends, and many that wanted to go deeper. Yet, I held them at arm's length, in fear.

What I found was this trauma was still affecting me as an adult. I had to understand that there was nothing about my childhood experience that was holding me back today. I was holding myself back. And the more I held myself back, the more my perpetrator was winning over me.

And I held the power to break the pain and escape the cage that was holding me back. And this freedom came by stopping the mental power this person had over my life. There was nothing he was doing in the present to hold me back—only I had that power. And with a mindset shift, I could be free.

This wasn't a "journey" to freedom. There was no place to go. Rather, it was a mental shift. And I was strong enough to make the shift.

Many of us have areas in our past that restrain us from forming open relationships with people around us. Perhaps, like my case, it's a childhood trauma. Perhaps it's our limited view of our self. Perhaps it's labels that authorities in our life have stuck on us. Perhaps it's parents that never believed in us. We all have our own limiting beliefs. And some are large enough to hold us back.

Are you comfortable being transparent with people around you? If not, what's holding you back? I encourage you to speak it. Identify it. But if it's holding you back, I suggest you find your own path to freedom.

There's so much joy on the other side, and I extend a hand for you to join me.

4. SHOW CONFIDENCE

Your audience will pick up on how you view yourself. If you lack confidence, they'll know. And if you're too confident, they'll notice that, too. Neither will serve you well. It's important that you establish your expertise. But you certainly don't want to do it in a boastful way. The trick is to frame your past success in terms of why it matters now. What role does it have to play in meeting your audience's objectives?

Your confidence can be contagious. It'll help build a mutual natural trust. You know what you're doing, and they'll take note. And they'll likely trust you. But you must also show an openness to continuing to learn.

As an expert in your field, if you can show your confidence along with a willingness to listen and grow, you'll likely score big on the trust meter.

5. BE TRUTHFUL

This sounds like a foregone conclusion, right? But, according to liespotting.com, human beings are lied to as many as 200 times a day.

In swearing-in ceremonies, you'll likely hear this affirmation on something similar: "I promise to tell the truth, the whole truth, and nothing but the truth." Being truly honest with your audience requires more than speaking simple truths. It requires giving them complete information. That may mean telling them things they don't want to hear. That's the whole truth.

6. MAKE PEOPLE FEEL SAFE

Creating a space that is safe seems to be a hot topic. We all have reasons not to trust others. Perhaps we've been burned in the past. Perhaps we've had business deals that have soured. Maybe the person we trusted lied to us.

I think the current national narrative around safe spaces is making people more open and aware about times when they didn't feel safe, and how that can affect one's life and the need to collectively create safe spaces. From sexual abuse by priests, business leaders, elected officials, and others, to a general feeling of anxiety, people too often just don't feel safe.

You can—to some degree—change that for your audience. Making your audience feel safe will impact their view of you and, ultimately, their trust. It's important to recognize boundaries, to know when it's time to show some reserve. You must respect personal space, which varies from person to person. Again, this underscores the importance of coming to know your audience and of an openness and willingness to listen.

7. SAY "NO" SOMETIMES

I admit this seems contradictory. We've talked about delivering, meeting your audience's needs, and filling gaps. But saying "no" can add to your credibility and build trust.

We discussed, earlier, the importance of sometimes saying no, in order to avoid overcommitting. Here's another reason to do so.

Imagine feeling chest pain, going to your primary care physician, and having your primary care physician offer to do open-heart surgery on you. I'd be taken back. How about you?

While working with your audience, there may be things that are outside of your core competency—your area of expertise. Trying to do everything is a sure-fire formula for disaster. You can't be everything to everyone. It just won't work.

So, when asked to do things that are not part of your area of expertise, offer to bring in another partner for that piece of the work. As long as you bring in a competent partner, you'll likely not disappoint your audience or lose trust. In fact, the trust factor will likely go up.

While working with clients, I tell them to pick two of these three: fast, quality, or cheap. When they ask for all three, I have to tell them it's not possible. I manage that upfront so that I don't disappoint.

The main point here is that you can't do everything and be everything for everyone. And acknowledging this fact up front likely won't hurt trust; it's likely to increase it.

8. BE OPEN TO FEEDBACK

I wish I did everything perfectly—every time. But the reality is, I don't. Neither do you. We'll make mistakes. We'll miss the mark. We'll have areas we haven't even thought about. Other people can add valuable feedback. Perhaps your audience can. So listen.

Being open to feedback and incorporating it, as appropriate, will most likely boost others' trust. If you think you know everything and the best way to do everything, you're likely only fooling yourself. Others will see that, and it will negatively impact their trust in you.

9. MAKE TIME

I'm guessing that previous generations didn't respond to the question, "How are you doing?" with, "Busy!" quite so often as we do today. But don't you long for a different response? Why are we so busy? We have more technology and aids than we ever have before. Shouldn't they be freeing up time?

I think we sometimes try to make ourselves feel important by telling people we're busy. After all, if we're busy, it suggests we're accomplishing things. And if we're accomplishing things, doesn't that make us important? And if we're important, certainly others should naturally trust us.

But not so fast.

In his book *Essentialism*, Greg McKeown builds an impressive case for doing less and doing it more thoroughly. My speaking coach referred this book to me after watching me try to juggle a million balls, as my ADHD often prompts me to do. And she's right—I am better served to do less and remain focused. So are you.

Among other things, doing less can allow us to spend more time with others. And making time for your audience will show you care and provide a mega dose of trust.

This would be a great time to look back at Chapter 7 titled "Making A Connection." How can you make time for your audience and, in doing so, create a deeper connection?

I can't tell you how to adjust your calendar, how to do more but to a greater degree—but I can tell you that, if you do, and if you make time for your audience, you can expect their trust in you to grow. So, too, will your ability to persuade. And isn't that the superpower we're all looking for?

10. BE RELIABLE

We've discussed delivering as promised, but there's a similar, yet different, concept, equally important to building trust: being reliable.

And for the sake of our conversation in this book, I'd say that reliability is the other nine tips working in concert, and without exception. It's the culmination; the product of the work you put in. It's the outcome of everything working harmoniously.

To recap: Without trust, nothing else in this book matters. It's the cornerstone for persuasion. So, before going back to Chapter 1, looking for ways to begin unleashing your superpower of persuasion, focus now on this chapter. This chapter matters the most. Without it, persuasion will never happen.

Another industry expert's perspective:

> When I first started out podcasting two-plus years ago, I remember three pieces of information I learned: The average podcast lasts seven episodes, the average number of downloads per episode is 150, and every podcaster has to help her audience "know, like, and trust" the host.
>
> I knew I could go well beyond seven podcast episodes, but I had no idea how many people would listen, much less know, like, and trust me. After all, I was on a mission to understand the complexities of health behavior change in the workplace and why our industry is so stuck.
>
> Knowing my subject matter was niche and my views were nontraditional in a very traditional industry, I wasn't going to be in the top of iTunes or garner the audience of Tim Ferris or *Freakonmics*. But still, I wanted to at least reach the average number of downloads per episode.
>
> So what did I do? Obsessively checked my stats, of course! I did this for quite a few months until, frankly, I didn't think it was productive anymore. I refocused on producing my show and hoped my message would resonate.
>
> Then something happened—I started getting a few emails from people who were thanking me for my podcast and my

message. They were tired of our industry not changing, as well, but felt they didn't have a voice in the matter. I wrote back to each and every one and even talked to a few on the phone. In fact, one has become a friend.

After going to an industry conference to speak, it was amazing meeting people who say they listen to my podcast. One guy even showed me that I was one of two podcasts he listened to.

Maybe I was on to something, but would they buy?

The true test of building an audience was selling a product (yes, for real money) that could help them challenge the status quo in their organizations. It was scary, but I proceeded to fill all seven small-group training spots!

As I look back over the two-plus years of hosting my podcast, there are three things I've done to build trust with my audience (even if I didn't know I was doing it):

Be your authentic self: I don't put on a front. I talk about my screwups, I ask guests questions that come up as we talk (instead of sticking to a script), and I talk about how hard it can be to challenge common thinking. I believe people are craving authenticity in a social media world that doesn't show the hard stuff.

Give until it hurts: There have been times when I'm staying up late to get a podcast episode out, responding to a post in my free Facebook group, or working on a new free guide, wondering if it's worth it. I mean, I'm a business owner. . . Shouldn't I start selling? The truth is that people will be more likely to buy from people they know, like, and trust. I guarantee I wouldn't have filled up my small-group training without giving out free (and valuable) content first.

Consistency: It takes a while for people to get to know you, much less trust you. Showing up when you say you will, delivering helpful content, and not disappearing when things get tough all build trust. In fact, about a year ago, I skipped a few weeks, as things got busy. A listener reached out to check if I was okay. That not only touched me but made me realize I needed to show up consistently. Now, every Wednesday, I publish a new podcast episode. If I'm going to take another hiatus, I'll be sure to tell them why I'm taking a breather.

Fast forward to current day, and I barely check my podcast stats. The last time I did, I'm getting the average downloads in one day instead of one month. My podcast audience continues to grow as my regular listeners recommend it to everyone they come across. Because they trust me, they are my best advertising.

Jen Arnold

RedesigningWellness.com

Ready for the next step? Let's talk about the importance of the greater good.

Questions for Reflection

1. Can you think of a time when someone broke trust with you? What happened? How did you feel?

2. This chapter identifies ten ways you can build trust. Of these, which ones are you strong in?

3. Of these ways to build trust, in which ones are you weak, and how?

4. How do you think you can improve your areas of weakness?

5. Have you broken the trust of someone in your life? How can you seek to repair it?

Chapter 13

THE GREATER GOOD

"For the good of the many, for the happiness of the many,
out of compassion for the world."

—Siddhārtha Gautama—

Now that you've come to better understand persuasive communications, let's return to where we began: the adoption of my daughter.

Completing an international adoption in a country in collapse, in six and a half months, is a pretty remarkable task. Admittedly, while in the middle of the process, it seemed like I would never find success, and success looked like bringing my daughter to American soil.

But it did end. Obstacles were overcome. Boundaries were destroyed. And I'd attained success.

After landing in Miami, I found myself standing in the airport concourse, stunned that this ordeal was over. And for a brief moment, I was proud; I had finally completed my mission to adopt this baby. I guess I did have reason to be happy with my work. After all, my new daughter arrived safely as a direct result of my efforts.

But within moments, the sense of accomplishment went out the window. The short-lived self-congratulations gave way to wonder.

I looked down at her as she whimpered. Turns out, she had double ear infections, and the cabin pressure of the plane had caused extreme pain.

As I looked at her, I began to wonder what her life would be like. Would she be a doctor and heal the sick? Would she be a teacher, educating hundreds of students who would then impact thousands of lives? Would she be a humanitarian and relieve suffering? Would she go back to Haiti to help her country of origin?

While, obliviously, I couldn't answer any of those questions, what I did now know was that my impact wasn't limited to the completion of the adoption.

The adoption was more like a stone being tossed into a lake or pond. You've done that, haven't you? Tossed a rock into the water? There's a deep sound as the rock impacts the water and begins heading to the bottom. Then, there are ripples that extend beyond the point of impact.

I now viewed my adoption as that rock entering the water. It was the genesis for ripples that would extend well beyond the point of impact. The good would extend well beyond my adoption as my new daughter began to change lives within her sphere.

This realization completely changed my thinking of my adoption and, by extension, my work in general.

It's easy for me to get focused on the daily details that it takes to keep my work going. There are emails, phone calls, meetings, deals to close, and goals to accomplish.

But there's something bigger; with a focus on helping others, my work will extend well beyond.

What is it that you're passionate about? What gets you out of bed? What gives you the energy?

Entrepreneurs aren't just building businesses. They create jobs, leading to a mom being able to provide for her family. Perhaps that looks like her son getting the tutoring he needs to find success in school. Can you imagine the possibilities?

Healthcare workers aren't just treating patients. Their work brings life to families and clarity during times of crisis. They heal young children, granting them a new lease on life. And then these children grow up and positively impact people around them.

Community activists aren't just rallying the troops. They are leading changes that have the potential to impact lives today and beyond. They are creating policy changes that can give marginalized groups new opportunities to succeed.

So, what is it that you do? What's your passion? Now, think big. How are you impacting lives beyond your daily activities?

My point is this: When we understand that our efforts have ripples of impact, we can move past all the things that slow or misdirect us.

With a focus on the greater good, you're unstoppable; your actions will impact lives well beyond what you can dream or imagine. And the superpower of persuasive communication is the tool that will help you change lives.

Grab your cape. There's work to be done! And you're the perfect person to do it.

ABOUT THE AUTHOR

Known to many as Mr. Persuasion, Jeff Tippett wrote the book on persuasive communications.

Speaking to international audiences through keynotes and seminars, Jeff helps attendees increase their effectiveness, gives them powerful tools to reach their goals, and empowers attendees to positively impact and grow their organizations or businesses.

His second book, slated for a January 2019 release, is titled: *Unleashing Your Superpower: Why Persuasive Communication Is The Only Force You Will Ever Need*. His bold statement is that we all live or die based on our ability to persuade.

In 2014, Jeff founded Targeted Persuasion, an award-winning public affairs + communications firm. He has worked with renowned brands like Airbnb, The National Restaurant Association, The League of Women Voters, The League of Conservation Voters, plus others. Other industry experts have validated Jeff's work with numerous awards including the prestigious The American Advertising Award.

The heart and soul of Jeff's presentations are the emotional story he tells of adopting his youngest daughter from Haiti while the country's government was collapsing. Through this near death experience of navigating civil unrest and institutional bureaucracy in a third world nation, Jeff learned valuable lessons on how to persuade others without ever manipulating. Jeff unpacks these secrets of the superpower of persuasion in every presentation.

CPSIA information can be obtained
at www.ICGtesting.com
Printed in the USA
FSHW011116260519

9 781733 533805